By Florence Theriault

Gold Horse Publishing

© Copyright 2008 Theriault's Gold Horse Publishing. All rights reserved.

No part of this book may be reproduced or utilized in any form or by any means, electronic or mechanical, including photocopying, recording, or by an information retrieval system, without permission, in writing, from the author or the publisher.

To order additional copies contact:
Dollmasters, PO Box 2319, Annapolis, MD 21404
Tel. 800-966-3655   Fax 410-571-9605
www.dollmasters.com

Art Direction & Design: Travis Hammond
Photography: Gerald Nelson
Production Design: Cindy Gonzalez
Conservation Department Director: Kristen Hadjoglou
Senior Conservator: Terry Lanford

$75
ISBN: 1-931503-49-4
Printed in Hong Kong

This antique doll collection auctioned by Theriault's of Annapolis, Maryland, January 5, 2008. *www.theriaults.com.*

The Geri Baker Collection

There are certain persons that, attending auctions, become the focus of that event. An anticipation races through the audience when that collector appears. For the past two decades, Geri Baker has been such a collector, presenting at each event with such force that her winning seemed a certainty. Sometimes, too, there has seemed such a casual air about her that collectors were heard to wonder if she really understood the specialness of the rare dolls that she gathered. It was an emotion that Geri, herself, reflected upon.

"I'm not sure yet if I'm a collector or just a storer. A mother or just a jailer. Or a romantic custodian!"

Not to worry.

For here has been a collector that has always known exactly what she was doing in her bidding choices, that studied dolls incessantly, that knew the special nature of each and every doll she decided to call "mine". Bravado was simply an actress face for emotions that every collector has felt as these entries from Geri Baker's private journal attest.

"I was shaking when they handed her to me at the auction. I have to admit bidding was fun, but winning was scary!"

"At that auction dolls were all going too high. I was scared I spent too much money so I let a princess go. As a consolation I won her sister and today she stands in a queenly manner. Yet I'll always remember the princess that got away."

It is appropriate as this collection now leaves her caring hands, that one further quote from her journal is shared. The quote was written, not yesterday, but at the beginning of her collecting years when she had just won, in classic Baker celebratory style, a doll from another's collection.

"I've realized that the passing on of these dolls is merely a passing of time. My dolls will grace time forever, where I can only hold them for a day."

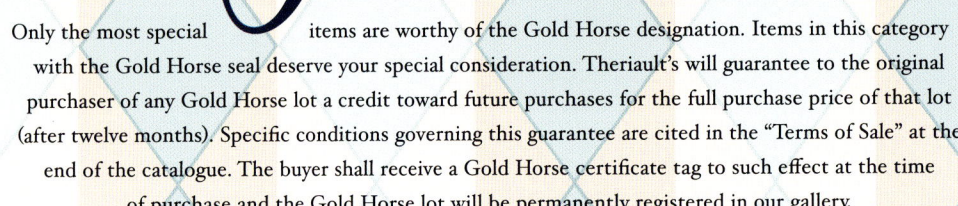

Gold Horses

Only the most special items are worthy of the Gold Horse designation. Items in this category with the Gold Horse seal deserve your special consideration. Theriault's will guarantee to the original purchaser of any Gold Horse lot a credit toward future purchases for the full purchase price of that lot (after twelve months). Specific conditions governing this guarantee are cited in the "Terms of Sale" at the end of the catalogue. The buyer shall receive a Gold Horse certificate tag to such effect at the time of purchase and the Gold Horse lot will be permanently registered in our gallery.

1. 11" An All-Original French Bisque Premiere Bebe Jumeau, Size 3
3. 28" A Spectacular French Bisque Bebe, Size 13, by Schmitt et Fils with Original Body
6. 13" Stunningly Beautiful French Bisque Bebe A.T., Size 3, by Thuillier
11. 10" Petite French Bisque Bebe Jumeau, Size 1, with Original Wig and Chemise
13. 22" Superb French Bisque Bebe Jumeau in original Jumeau Couturier Costume
14. 28" Beautiful Brown-Eyed Bebe Jumeau Triste, Size 13, in Original Costume
15. 10" Wonderful Petite French Bisque Bebe E.J., Size 2, by Jumeau With Brown Eyes
41. 24" Outstanding and Extremely Rare French Bisque Bebe "H" by Halopeau
41.1. 11" Rare Petite Model Bebe by Joanny, Size 2, with Fine Antique Costume
42. 35" Outstanding Grand French Bisque Bebe, Size 13, by Leon Casimir Bru
43. 15" Very Rare French Bisque Double-Faced Poupee by Leon Casimir Bru, Depose Model
44. 18" French "Bebe Gourmand" by Leon Casimir Bru with Provenance and Trousseau
46. 19" German Bisque Character "Gretchen" by K*R with Outstanding Sculpting
47. 12" German Bisque POuty Character, "Marie" by Kammer and Reinhardt
48. 20" German Bisque Portrait Lady, 152, by Simon and Halbig
49. 22" Extremely Rare French Bisque Artist Doll by Albert Marque with Original Body
59. 24" Outstanding Bebe Triste by Emile Jumeau in Superb Original Costume and Box
60. 24" Superb Earliest Period French Bisque Bebe EJ, Size 9 with Fine Antique Costume
62. 14" Extremely Rare French Wooden Court Doll Portraying Marie Antoinette
78. 16" French Bisque Portrait Poupee in Original Hunting Costume with Accessories
81. 18" Exceptionally Rare French Bisque Poupee by Dehors with Portrait Face
82. 11" Bisque Bebe Brevete, Size 6/0, by Leon Casimir Bru with Signed Shoes and Bonnet
83. 18" An Outstanding French Bisque Bebe A.T. by Thuillier with Signed A.T. Shoes
85. 28" Outstanding French Bisque Bebe by Leon Casimir Bru, Size 11, with Signed Shoes
88. 14" German Bisque Pouting Character, 7759, by Gebruder Heubach
89. 14" Rare German Bisque Character by Bahr and Proschild for Swaine & Co
92. Germany 26" Large German Bisque Toddler "Erika" by Simon and Halbig
103. 18" Rare German Bisque Character, 1488, by Simon and Halbig
104. 12" Wonderful German Bisque Character, 1498, with Sculpted Hair
105. 12" Petite German Bisque Character, 185, with Glass Eyes by Kestner
108. 22" Outstanding German Bisque Lady with Smile, Model 1388, by Simon and Halbig
123. 15" Fine French Early Model Poupee by Leon Casimir Bru with Trunk and Trousseau
124. 26" Grand French Bisque Bebe A.T., Size 15, by Thuillier
129. 22" French Bebe Triste by Emile Jumeau with Early Costume and Signed Jumeau Shoes
131. 25" Very Rare French Bisque Bebe E.J.A. with Original Costume and Box
144. 17" Extremely Rare French Bisque "Statuette-Poupee" by Radiguet & Cordonnier
145. 13" Beautiful French Bisque Bebe Bru Jne, Size 2, by Leon Casimir Bru with Bru Shoes
156. 18" French Bisque Bebe, size 6, by Leon Casimir Bru with Signed Shoes
161. 20" Very Rare Swiss Studio Doll by Sasha Morgenthaler

183. 40" Bebe Jumeau, Incised Depose, in Grand Size 20 with Antique Costume
184. 42" French Bisque Block Letter Bebe by Gaultier in Size 16 with Original Body
189. 19" Rare German Bisque Character, 141, by Hertel and Schwab
192. 24" French Bisque Bebe Jumeau, Size 11, with Original Chemise and Shoes
195. 11" Petite French Bisque Bebe Jumeau, Size 2, in Original Chemise
196. 25" French Bisque Bebe Jumeau, in Original Costume with Decorative Box
198. 15" German Bisque Toddler, "Phillip", 115/A, by Kammer and Reinhardt
202. 16" Very Rare German Bisque Characters, "Max" and "Moritz" by K*R
205. Germany 18" Compelling and Rare German Art Character Doll by Marian Kaulitz
223. 16" Splendid French Bisque Bebe A.T. by Andre Thuillier with Bisque Hands
229. 11" Petite French Bisque Bebe Steiner, Figure A, in Original Au Nain Bleu Costume
231. 13" Very Rare French Bisque Taufling Baby by Jules Steiner
232. 35" French Bisque Bebe Steiner, Figure C in Grand 35" Size, with Bisque Hands
240. 26" French Bisque Bebe E.J., Size 12, with Original Jumeau Couturier Costume
241. 18" Beautiful French Bisque Poupee with All-Wooden Articulated Body
254. 26" Rare Grand-Size French Bisque Pouting Character, 252, by SFBJ
258. 16" Rare German Brown-Complexioned Bisque Character, 1358, by Simon and Halbig
260. 12" Beautiful German Brown-Complexioned Bisque Doll Known as "A.T. Kestner"
261. 21" Very Fine French Bisque Bebe Brevete by Leon Casimir Bru
262. 19" Beautiful French Bisque Portrait Bebe by Jumeau
263. 22" Gorgeous French Bisque Poupee by Pierre-Francois Jumeau with Wooden Arms
264. 19" Lovely French Bisque Bebe by Schmitt & Fils with Original Lambswool Wig
267. 37" Very Rare Grand-Sized French Bisque Bebe, Series C, by Jules Steiner
268. 22" French Bisque Portrait Bebe by Jumeau with Rare Expression
270. 14" French Bisque Poupee by Jumeau in Superb Original Turkish Exhibition Costume
301. 18" German Bisque Painted Eye Character by Kestner
302. 15" Rare German Bisque Character, 207, by Catterfelder Puppenfabrik
306. 18" Rare German Bisque Character, 520, by Bahr and Proschild for Kley and Hahn
307. 24" German Bisque Pouty, "Phillip" by Kammer and Reinhardt in Fine Larger Size
310. 12" Pouting Character, 115A , by Kammer and Reinhardt with Loved Teddy Bear
311. 31" German Bisque Child, 1269, by Simon & Halbig in Original Costume
337. 24" Outstanding French Bisque Earliest Period EJ, Size 11
338. 15" Early French Bisque Bebe Schmitt, Size 1, Known as "Cup and Saucer" Style
341. 42" Rare French Bisque Block Letter Bebe by Gaultier in Size 16
347. 26" Very Beautiful French Bisque Bebe E.J. by Jumeau, Size 12
348. 32" French Bisque "Eden Bebe", Size 16, with Character Expression
353. 34" Very Large French Bisque Bebe Steiner, Figure A, Size 20
355. 9" Small German Bisque Character, "Hans" by Kammer and Reinhardt

1. An All-Original French Bisque Premiere Bébé Jumeau, Size 3

11" (28 cm.) Pressed bisque socket head with shy-faced expression, brown glass enamel inset eyes in small eye socket cuts, delicately painted brows and lashes, dark eyeliner, accented nostrils and eye corners, closed mouth with outlined lips, pierced ears, blonde mohair wig over cork pate, French composition and wooden eight-loose-ball jointed body with straight wrists. Condition: generally excellent. Marks: 3 (head) Jumeau Medaille d'Or Paris (body). Comments: Emile Jumeau, his premiere model bébé, 1878. Value Points: in superbly preserved original condition, with very sweet classic expression, fine bisque, original wig, original early body with fine original finish, and wearing all original Jumeau couturier costume of aqua silk satin with Alencon lace, matching bonnet, original muslin Jumeau chemise, undergarments, Jumeau knit stockings and black leather shoes with silk rosettes signed "E. Jumeau Med d'or Paris." $7500/9500

2. French All-Bisque Mignonette in Original Presentation Case

3.5" (9 cm.) doll. 6" x 3" case. A heavy card-paper valise with decorative paper covers and strap handles, hinges open to reveal an all-bisque mignonette with swivel head, painted facial features, jointed arms and legs, painted blue slippers, blonde fleecy wig, wearing original lacy dress. Still tied to the original paper lining of the valise are two additional dresses with lacy accessories. Condition: generally excellent. Comments: French, circa 1885. Value Points: perfectly preserved luxury presentation doll and her costumes. $800/1200

3. A Spectacular French Bisque Bébé, Size 13, by Schmitt et Fils with Original Body

28" (71 cm.) Pressed bisque socket head with pear-shaped facial modeling, very plump cheeks, almond shaped eye sockets, brown glass paperweight inset eyes, thick dark eyeliner, painted lashes, mauve blushed eye shadow, widely arched brush-stroked brows with feathered detail, accented eye corners, shaded nostrils, closed mouth with defined space between the outlined lips, pierced ears, dimpled chin and cheek corners, blonde mohair wig over cork pate, French composition and wooden eight-loose-ball-jointed body with flat-cut derriere base, straight wrists, beautifully costumed in antique silk and lace dress, matching bonnet, undergarments, knit stockings, ivory silk shoes. Condition: generally excellent. Marks: SCH (in shield) 13 (on head). (also marked SCH on derriere). Comments: Schmitt et Fils, circa 1884. Value Points: superb quality of sculpting with wonderfully defined features, finest quality bisque and painting, original body and body finish. $18,000/27,000

6. Stunningly Beautiful French Bisque Bébé A.T., Size 3, by Thuillier

13" (33 cm.) Pressed bisque swivel head on kid-edged bisque shoulder plate, large pale blue glass paperweight eyes with brilliant color and depth, dark eyeliner, delicately painted lashes, rose blushed eye shadow, brush-stoked and feathered brows, accented nostrils and eye corners, closed mouth with defined space between the outlined lips, pierced ears, blonde mohair wig over cork pate, kid bébé body with gusset-jointing at elbows, hips and knees, bisque lower arms and hands, wearing antique ice blue silk ensemble, undergarments, stockings, leather shoes signed "3". Condition: generally excellent, one finger of left hand is restored. Marks: A. 3 T. (head) 3 (left shoulder) A.T. (right shoulder). Comments: Thuillier, circa 1882, the first period model of his illustrious bébé. Value Points: the rarity of the early period A.T. kid-bodied bébé in this small size is further enhanced by its stunning beauty, exemplary sculpting, bisque and painting, spectacular eyes, original sturdy body. $25,000/35,000

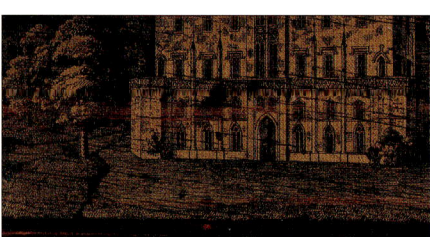

4. Rare Early Doll-Sized Secretaire with Gilded Chateau Scene in the Biedermeier Style

13" (33 cm.) Ebony-finished secretaire features a curved front flat writing table with cubicle back edged by matching cabinets with oval shaped mirrored doors, cabriole shaped legs, and four drawers. The secretaire is decorated with gilded floral and scroll scenes, and on the desk top is a rich scene of a large castle with turrets and a waving flag. Excellent condition. Germany, circa 1885, a rare size of the so-called Biedermeier furniture, probably G.H. Wagner & Sohn, perfect for display with small bébé as classic poupée, and with rare decorations. $1100/1600

5. 19th Century Miniature with Hand-painted Scenes

3" (8 cm.) A silver-framed miniature sailing ship with turning wheeled base and movable waving flag is decorated with hand-painted enamel scenes depicting children and romantic couples in country and seaside scenes. There are ten different people featured in the scenes, and the detail of decoration includes both sides of the sail and the underside of the ship as well as the ship sides. Excellent condition. Late 19th century, a rare model of the miniature art. $400/500

7. French Paper Mache Poupée with Original Folklore Costume of Arles
10" (25 cm.) Paper mache shoulder head with oval-shaped face and elongated throat of adult woman, black enamel eyes, painted short lashes and feathered brows, accented nostrils, slightly parted lips with double row of teeth, black painted pate with hand-tied brunette hair, kid body with shapely torso and limbs, stitched and separated fingers. Condition: generally excellent, body especially sturdy. Comments: French, circa 1850. Value Points: in beautifully preserved condition, the elegant lady is wearing her well-detailed original folklore costume of fine silks and laces, including embroidered lace coiffe and tulle sous-sleeves; the doll is featured in *The Encyclopedia of French Dolls* by Theimer, page 445. $2500/3500

8. Early Miniature Dresden Paper Clock and Floral Arrangements in Original Glass Domes
3.5" (9 cm.) Comprising an exquisite faux-clock with central face (without numerals) is constructed of gilded paper with suspended paper pendulum, flanked by glass crystal columns, and rested upon a gilded paper base; along with a pair of paper floral arrangements with a variety of delicately cut paper flowers arranged in embossed gilded paper vases. Each of the three pieces is presented in its original blown glass dome on ebony-finished wooden base. Excellent condition. A very rare miniature ensemble, circa 1860. $800/1200

9. Outstanding French Paper Mache Poupée in Original Folklore Costume of Arles
20" (51 cm.) Solid domed paper mache shoulder head of adult woman with oval-shaped face and elongated strong throat, small black enamel glass eyes, painted lashes and brows, accented nostrils of aquiline nose, closed mouth with small prim lips, original brunette hand-tied human hair wig over black painted pate, shapely kid poupée body with gusset-jointed hips, stitched and separated fingers. Condition: generally excellent, body especially sturdy. Comments: French, circa 1860, the wonderfully preserved early poupée has fine lustrous original patina of complexion, original wig, body, and superb original costume of wealthy lady of Arles highlighted by silk fichu with Alencon lace edged with pearl and glass bead teardrops, pearls, and black velvet coiffe. $2500/3500

10. Delightful and Rare French Mechanical Pull-Toy "Polichinelle Riding an Ostrich"

24" (61 cm.) overall h. 16"l. of base. A bisque-headed Polichinelle doll is seated upon a large paper mache ostrich. The doll has blue glass paperweight inset eyes, painted features, closed mouth with piquant smile, pierced ears, blonde mohair wig over cork pate, carton torso with classic Polichinelle front and back torso humps, carved wooden hands and feet, wearing blue and rose silk Polichinelle costume, and the ostrich has glass eyes and realistically painted and sculpted features and beak. The doll and ostrich are posed upon a metal wheeled wooden platform that hides a simple mechanism; when pulled along Polichinelle quickly turns his head from side to side, and waves the ostrich forward with the baton in his hand. Condition: generally excellent. Comments: the maker of the distinctive French painted platform pull-toys remains a mystery; the doll head is from Jumeau, circa 1880. Value Points: absolutely delightful and rare toy with luxurious and imaginative details. $6000/9000

11. Petite French Bisque Bébé Jumeau, Size 1, with Original Wig

10" (25 cm.) Bisque socket head with creamy bisque, large brown glass paperweight inset eyes, lushly painted lashes, brushstroked and feathered brows, accented nostrils, closed mouth with outlined lips, pierced ears, blonde mohair wig over cork pate, French composition and wooden fully-jointed body. Condition: generally excellent. Marks: Depose Tete Jumeau Bte SGSDG 1 (head, and artist checkmarks) Jumeau Medaille d'Or Paris (body). Comments: Emile Jumeau, circa 1888. Value Points: very beautiful brown-eyed bébé with original waist-length wig, original Jumeau muslin chemise, earrings, original body finish. $4000/5500

12. French Accessories for Poupée on Original Card and Gift Box

7" (18 cm.) x 5" box. The heavy paper card with gilt stenciled edging and label "Nouveaute Paris" presents original accessories and toiletries for classic French poupée or small bébé. Included are decorative comb, brushes and hair comb, sachet, powder jar and "extrait d'odeur" in fancy glass bottle. The card is laid in original gift box with gilt edging. Very good condition, some card spotting, contents excellent. French, circa 1880. $700/1000

13. Superb French Bisque Bébé Jumeau in Original Jumeau Couturier Costume

22" (56 cm.) Bisque socket head, blue glass paperweight inset eyes, dark painted eyeliner, painted lashes, rose blushed eye shadow, widely arched brush-stroked and feathered brows, accented nostrils, closed mouth with defined space between the outlined lips, pierced ears, blonde mohair wig over cork pate, French composition and wooden fully-jointed body. Condition: generally excellent. Marks: Depose Tete Jumeau Bte SGDG 10 (and artist checkmarks on head) Jumeau Medaille d'Or Paris (body). Comments: Emile Jumeau, circa 1888. Value Points: superb original condition of the creamy-complexioned bébé with beautiful painting, virtually unplayed with, having Jumeau studios couturier costume of pale rose silk and delicate laces and cord trim, undergarments, bonnet, Jumeau earrings, knit stockings and pale rose kid slippers with silk rosette medallions signed "E.Jumeau Med d'or Paris 1878" and "10". $6500/8500

14. Beautiful Brown-Eyed Bébé Jumeau Triste, Size 13, in Original Costume
28" (71 cm.) Pressed bisque socket head, brown glass paperweight inset eyes, thick dark eyeliner, delicately painted curly lashes, brush-stroked brows with feathered detail, accented eye corners, shaded nostrils, closed mouth with defined space between the outlined lips, separately applied pierced ears, brunette waist-length mohair wig over cork pate, French composition and wooden body with plump limbs and straight wrists. Condition: generally excellent. Marks: 13 (and artist check marks, head) Jumeau Medaille d'Or Paris (body). Comments: Emile Jumeau, circa 1885, his wistful faced child known as Bébé Triste. Value Points: very fine detail of sculpting featuring plump cheeks and dimpled chin, impressed dimples at lip corners and philtrum, lovely bisque and painting enhancing the rich brown eyes, original body and body finish, wearing original blue/grey silk faille dress with velvet trim, velvet bonnet, undergarments, black leather shoes and knit stockings. $15,000/20,000

15. Wonderful Petite French Bisque Bébé E.J., Size 2, by Jumeau With Brown Eyes
0" (0 cm.) Bisque socket head with pale bisque complexion, full cheeks, large brown glass paperweight inset eyes, dark lushly painted lashes, arched brush-stroked brows, accented nostrils, closed mouth with richly shaded lips, pierced ears, lambswool fleecy wig over cork pate, French composition fully-jointed body with straight wrists. Condition: generally excellent. Marks: Depose E. 2 J (head) Jumeau Medaille d'Or Paris (body). Comments: Emile Jumeau, circa 1884. Value Points: very beautiful petite bébé with entrancing large brown eyes contrasting the creamy pale complexion, original body and body finish, lovely early maroon silk and lace costume, undergarments, velvet bonnet, original silk "Bébé Jumeau" armband, original Jumeau socks, one original signed Jumeau shoe. $4500/6500

16. French Doll's "Chaise Brisee" with Gold Leaf Finish
14" (36 cm.) overall length. The wooden-framed "chaise brisee" has original gold leaf finish, classic short arms, cabriole style legs, elegantly curved back, and is upholstered in maroon patterned silk. Excellent condition. French, circa 1880, a rarely found doll-sized furniture model. $700/900

17. French Porcelain Poupée "Blondinette" by Adelaide Huret in Brown Velvet Ensemble

17" (43 cm.) Porcelain shoulder head with rounded childlike shape, pale complexion with delicate shading of cheeks and chin, modeled eyelids above painted blue eyes with shaded detail, thick black upper eyeliner, painted short lashes, lightly feathered brows, accented nostrils and eye corners, closed mouth with accented lips, original blonde astrakhan wig, gutta percha body with dowel and pin-jointed articulations, sculpted bisque hands. Condition: generally excellent, the head, wig, kid collarette and bisque hands are perfect, the body has some typical restoration. Marks: Huret Boul. Haussman Paris (stamp on kid collarette). Comments: Adelaide Huret, circa 1863. The doll, named Blondinette Davranches by her young owner, Pauline, lived at the wealthy Davranches family estate on 14 rue d'Ecuisse in Rouen, France and the Chateau de Bois l'Evique for 130 years. In 1863 Pauline wrote two letters to Blondinette on the doll's miniature stationery that bore the monogram "B". Remarkably the tiny envelopes were postmarked Paris and actually posed to the family homes where, presumably, Blondinette waited for her young mistress to return. Those letters, along with postmarked envelopes, an original photograph of Blondinette posed with her furniture (see lots 18 & 19) and a publicity brochure "La Ronde des Toileries" from the boutique of Mlle Bereaux are included with the doll. In 1994, the Chateau de Bois was closed, its contents dispersed, and discovered in a corner of the attic was a storage chest containing Blondinette and her perfectly preserved trousseau. The doll and her trousseau were presented by Theriault's in 1994 in a landmark auction "The Trousseau of Blondinette Davranche". It is that doll and many of her costumes, accessories and furniture that are offered in lot 17 and subsequent lots. Value Points: Historically important, Blondinette Davranche bears documented provenance, enhancing the classic beauty of the signature French poupée; her bisque hands are rare features, and the the doll wears a superb brown silk velveteen ensemble decorated with silk ribbons and gold beads, undergarments, leather slippers, and a fine bonnet, all elements of her original trousseau, and carries a brown silk/wool cape with soutache embroidery and black silk lace trim. $18,000/25,000

18. Blondinette's Fruitwood and Bronze Secretaire from Maison Giroux

11"h. table. 12"h. chair. Of finest cherry wood with striped maple wood inlays, the slant front desk features voluptuously curved apron and cabriole legs and is trimmed with an abundance of richly sculpted bronze mounts and beaded edging. The drawers have bronze pulls, as does the fitted interior and there is a rose velvet writing surface. Condition: generally excellent. Marks: Maison Alph. Giroux, Paris (paper label). Comments: commissioned for the exclusive Parisian mid-19th century shop, the desk was once owned by the Huret poupée Blondinette and is shown in the original photograph of Blondinette on her family-owned estate in Rouen, France. Value Points: superb workmanship of the finely crafted miniature desk, sized for display with classic 45 cm poupée, with Giroux label, and with important provenance. $4500/6500

Detail #18.

19. Blondinette's Gold-Lead Cast Iron Salon Table and Chair by Huret

11"h. 10"w. 6"d. Each with cast iron frame with scrolled and spiral ornamentation and rich gold-lead hand-applied finish, the chair with elegantly curved arms and oval-shaped back, and the table with a single pedestal terminating in a tripod base with elegant scrolls joined by gilded spindles with a centered finial. Both chair and table are upholstered in original luxurious dark green velvet, the table with gold tack edging above long green fringe. Each bears the maker's green stamp "Maison Huret, No. 22 Boulevard Montmartre Paris" as well as the unique gold lettered registry number: table 9874 (?) and chair 198 (?). Both the chair and the table are depicted in the photograph of Blondinette Davranche presumably at the Chateau de Bois gardens. The story of the furniture is told in the 1994 book "The Trousseau of Blondinette Davranches". Superb original condition of the rare furniture. Circa 1863. $5000/8500

20. Blondinette's Black Silk Taffeta Gown
The crisp, yet soft, black silk taffeta evening or ball gown has an interwoven leaf design, fitted bodice and waist, low cut neckline, three tiered flared sleeved to just above the elbow, and an attached extended collar that criss-crosses over the bodice before tying at the back and extending the back length of the skirt. The gown is decorated with narrow black silk zig-zag ribbons and lace medallions. The gown is muslin lined and completely hand-stitched in the tiniest of stitches. Near mint condition. Circa 1863. $1200/1800

21. Blondinette's Black Taffeta Paletot
Of lustrous soft black silk taffeta the hip length jacket features a fitted waist and flared hips. The front is smoothly fitted, and there is a four-panel full back, full rounded collar and tapered length full sleeves. The jacket is trimmed with lavender silk braid edged with black silk loop piping. Near mint condition. Circa 1863. $600/900

22. Blondinette's Velvet Evening Purse with Metallic Trim and Belt, Gold Coins
Luxurious velvet evening purse is a rich shade of fuchsia with matching fuchsia silk accordion sides and lining, contains six tiny gold and silver coins. The purse is trimmed with ribbed pattern gold metallic banding and clasp, with matching belt loops dotted with gold studs, and has a matching belt with two size adjustments. The purse is presented in its original box with label of Mlle Bereux, an original dressmaker for Huret who later opened her own couturiere poupée shop nearby to the Huret establishment. Near mint condition. 1860s. $1800/2500

23. Blondinette's Black Silk Belt with Silver Figural Buckles
The 3/4" wide belt of black silk grosgrain has a pair of cast silver buckles with raised profile silhouettes depicting Napoleon III and

Imperatrice Eugenie. The buckles are designed to be clasped together in symbolic unity. A very rare poupée accessory. Excellent condition. Circa 1865 $400/500

24. Blondinette's Blue Woolen and Ivory Silk Ensemble from Mlle Bereux in Original Box
The dart-shaped hip-length crisp ivory silk taffeta jacket with scalloped hem is edged in black velvet with black velvet buttons, and rests atop a blue lightweight woolen skirt with soutache trim that is overlaid with a 3/4 length paneled overskirt of ivory silk. The skirt overlay has the effect of an elongated jacket yet is actually an attached element of the skirt. The ensemble is presented in its original store box bearing the label of Mlle Bereux, the noted Parisian doll costume couturier whose story is told in *The Encyclopedia of French Dolls*. Near mint condition. Paris, circa 1863. $1200/1700

25. Blondinette's Turquoise Jewelry
The matched set of jewelry features tiny turquoise glass beads interspered with tiny gold beads, and includes a necklace with gold ormolu drop and gilded cross, two matching double-band bracelets, gilded watch with a trio of turquoise bead bangles and a daisy-shaped brooch, and a pair of gilded earrings with turquoise drops. Excellent condition. Circa 1863. $400/600

26. Blondinette's Summer Gown
Of crisp yet sheer white cotton, the gown features short flared sleeves with ruffled and scalloped edging that is repeated in the elongated collar that rounds the back neckline and forms into an extended length criss-cross at the front bodice. The tightly gathered skirt has four tiers of gathers that are edged by scalloping finished in overcast silk thread. The dress is, at once, airy and voluminous. Circa 1863. Near mint condition. $1200/1800

27. Blondinette's Blue Silk Plaid Gown
The gown is created in a striped/plaid printed silk faille fabric of cream and royal blue and features pouf sleeves with fitted arm bands, fitted bodice and waist, and box-pleated skirt. A large rounded collar at the back forms into two wide lappets that form a V-shaped decoration at the front. The collar, neckline and cuffs are edged in blue piping. The gown is fully muslin lined and has tiny pearl button and thread loop closures. Circa 1863. Near mint condition. $1100/1500

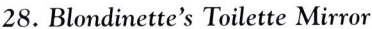

28. Blondinette's Toilette Mirror
The maple-wood framed oval mirror, designed to sit upon a toilette table, is arranged within a bracket hinged frame, and has an unusual arched leg support which can be folded flat, should Blondinette wish to pack the mirror for travel. Excellent condition. Circa 1863. $400/600

29. Blondinette's Fruitwood Ink Stand
1.5" (4 cm.) Of finest wood, the shell-carved ink stand has pen holder and wooden faux-pen, and two small blown glass ink holders. The ink stand is shown in the original vintage photograph of Blondinette seated at her desk at the family estate in Rouen, France. Circa 1863. Excellent condition. $400/500

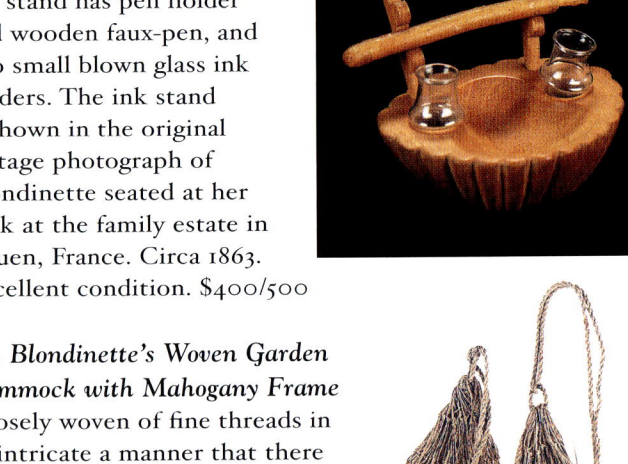

30. Blondinette's Woven Garden Hammock with Mahogany Frame
Loosely woven of fine threads in so intricate a manner that there are tiny knots at each juncture, the hammock, specifically scaled for a 45 cm. doll, is supported by artisan-crafted mahogany curved frames with carved holes for insertion of seven cords. The hammock is finished with woven braids at either end, edged by tassels with beehive woven designs. Near mint condition. Circa 1863. $600/900

31. Blondinette's Garden-Green Woven Hammock with Original Box
Very loosely woven hammock of strong silk threads in rich forest green colors have curved bone frames (one broken with small missing piece), and rope and tassel trim at each end. The hammock is contained in its original white gift box with gold edging identical to boxes from the prestigious doll shop of Au Caliphe de Bagdad where other accessories for Blondinette had been purchased, circa 1863. $500/800

32. Blondinette's Black Cashmere Riding Ensemble
Of superbly soft black cashmere, the two-piece ensemble features an extended length skirt designed for riding side-saddle, along with a matching elongated jacket with fitted waist and flared hips that match the pagoda-shaped sleeves. The ensemble is neatly trimmed with black silk cording and silk ball tassels. Near mint condition. Circa 1863. $1800/2600

33. Blondinette's Riding Crop with Carved Figural Handle
The delicately scaled riding crop features spiral handle with brass frame and a carved bone hand grip depicting basset hound head. The crop is fashioned to have flexibility in the exact manner as a full-sized crop, and there is an authentic delicate rope twist at the tip. Near mint condition. Circa 1863. $1500/2200

35. Blondinette's Petit Point Slippers and Needlework Sac
Each is composed of intricate and delicately colorful petit point patterns, the sac with woven braid handles and edging, and a maroon silk twill base and draw-string inner sac; and the slippers with tacked-on soft leather soles, padded silk lining, and silk pleated ruffle around the edges. Near mint condition. Circa 1863. $700/1000

34. Blondinette's Bed Chamber Costumes
Comprising a night robe of softest teal blue and cream flannel with matching detachable cape for chilly nights, and blue silk waist ties; along with a knitted silk/wool shawl in matching colors and matching slippers; and with a fine white cotton night shift with lace-edged button yoke and lace-edged cuffs. Near mint condition. Circa 1863. $1000/1500

36. Blondinette's Undergarments
Comprising two white cotton chemises, two petticoats, one pantalets, wired hoop, muslin sous-sleeves, cap, face veil, and a silk corset with yellow silk threads. Each piece features delicate hand-stitching. Near mint condition. Circa 1863. $600/900

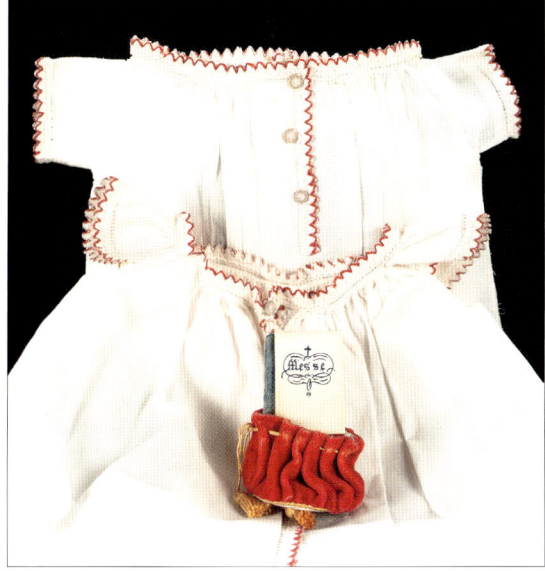

37. Blondinette's Chemises, Mass-book and Velvet Reticule
Of crisp white cotton, comprising a chemisette with tucks and yoke button closure, along with a gathered pinafore, each trimmed with scalloped edge detailed with red overcast stitching; along with a silk-bottom velvet reticule with gold thread ties containing Blondinette's rose-lined miniature Mass book. Near mint condition. Circa 1863. $500/800

38. Blondinette's Red Leather Sac du Voyage in Original Box
Of red leather with embossed pattern, the sac du voyage is fashioned in the classic manner with separate opening compartments at the purse-shaped top and box-shaped base. The top section features a silver clasp with red leather straps, and the bottom hard-sided section with V-shaped flap closure with brass hook, contains a small mirror. The sac du voyage is contained in its original box with red paper edging. Near mint condition. Circa 1863. $1500/2100

39. Blondinette's Embroidered Shawl and Carved Wooden Clogs
Of very fine silk wool blend, the rich red shawl with fringed edging has embroidered silk flowers and trailing vines. Along with wooden clogs with carved wooden heels and carved design, leather straps, and with green leather purse with twill belt loop and red leather lining. Excellent condition. Circa 1863. $800/1200

40. Blondinette's White Pique Gown and Silk Bonnet
Of very narrow vertically ribbed pique the gown features a fitted bodice with short capped sleeves and rounded neckline, flared skirt, scalloped edging with overcast stitching around the hem, neckline, sleeves, skirt panels and forming a detachable belt. Along with a silk wire-framed bonnet with silk thread edging and ivory silk ribbons and streamers. Circa 1863. Excellent condition. $800/1100

41. Outstanding and Extremely Rare French Bisque Bébé "H" by Halopeau

24" (61 cm.) Pressed bisque socket head with very full modeling of cheeks, dark blue paperweight inset eyes, thick dark eyeliner, painted lashes with dot highlights, brush-stroked and multi-feathered brows, accented eye corners, shaded nostrils of finely shaped nose, closed mouth with defined space between the shaded and outlined lips, pierced ears, blonde mohair wig over cork pate, French composition and wooden fully-jointed body with straight wrists, expressively posed fingers, wearing midnight blue velvet dress with ivory silk bodice, lace bonnet, undergarments, leather shoes, knit stockings. Condition: generally excellent. Marks: 4 H. Comments: Aristide Halopeau, circa 1878, successor to the Barrois doll firm, commissioned a unique sculpture for his bébé and commissioned its production by the Frayon porcelain firm with painting by the well-known French artist, Barnard. The creation of the bébé was purely a luxury and few models were made. This example appears in *The Encyclopedia of French Dolls*, page 270, and was acquired by Geri Baker from the Mildred Seeley Collection. $40,000/50,000

41.1. Rare Petite Model Bébé by Joanny, Size 2, with Fine Antique Costume

11" (28 cm.) Bisque socket head, deep blue glass paperweight inset eyes, painted lashes, brush-stroked and feathered brows, accented nostrils and eye corners, closed mouth with outlined lips, pierced ears, blonde mohair wig over cork pate, early French composition and wooden eight-loose-ball-jointed body with straight wrists. Condition: generally excellent. Marks: J 2. Comments: Joanny, circa 1885, the small firm created luxury bébés at its establishment on the prestige address of 202 Rue de Rivoli in Paris. Value Points: signed models of the distinctively sculpted Joanny bébés are very rare, this body particularly so in petite size, and wearing a beautiful antique costume, undergarments, kid slippers, original wig. $4000/5500

42. Outstanding Grand French Bisque Bébé, Size 13, by Leon Casimir Bru

35" (89 cm.) Pressed bisque swivel head on kid-edged bisque shoulder plate with modeled bosom and shoulder blades, large brown glass paperweight inset eyes, thick black eyeliner, painted lashes, slightly modeled brush-stroked brows with feathered detailing, accented eye corners, shaded nostrils, pierced ears, brunette human hair over cork pate, kid bébé body with scalloped-edge collarette, Chevrot jointed hips, wooden lower legs and feet, kid over wooden upper arms, bisque lower arms with separately sculpted fingers, wearing antique lace dress, undergarments, fancy bonnet. Condition: generally excellent, right finger reglued. Marks: 13 (head) Bru Jne 13 (shoulders). Comments: Leon Casimir Bru, circa 1884. Value Points: outstanding model of Bru's bébé from his Golden Age, in rarest large size that enhances the stunning sculpting, enhanced by suggestion of tiny tongue tip, dimpled chins, modeling of brows, very beautiful hands, and superb original condition. $30,000/40,000

43. Very Rare French Bisque Double-Faced Poupée by Leon Casimir Bru, Depose Model

15" (38 cm.) Solid domed bisque swivel head with flat-cut neck socket on bisque shoulder plate, sculpted facial model on both sides of heads depicting alternate moods of happiness and despair, each with painted facial features; one face with sculpted frown lines, squinting eyes and closed mouth modeled as though open and crying, painted details include tiny beaded teeth and "frowning" brows; the other face with a beaming smile, sculpted laughter crinkles around the eyes, impressed dimples, painted graceful brows and tiny beaded teeth. The head pivots easily side to side and the wig pivots horizontally from an axis at the level of the ear to reveal either face one at a time, with the wig hiding the alternate face. The poupée has deposed model of Bru kid lady body with square cut collarette, gusset jointing, shapely torso, and wooden arms with dowel articulation at shoulders, elbows and wrists, separately sculpted fingers, wearing fine antique gown, undergarments, leather boots, and double strand of early pearls. Condition: generally excellent. Comments: Leon Casimir Bru, the earliest version of his 1867 depose which he named "poupée surprise"; the patent illustration is shown in *The Bru Book* by Theimer/Theriault, and was made for one or two years only. Value Points: very rare model with superb quality of bisque and painting, original Bru body with wooden articulated arms, lovely costume. $15,000/20,000

44. Exceptionally Rare French Bisque "Bébé Gourmand" by Leon Casimir Bru with Provenance and Trousseau

18" (46 cm.) Pressed bisque swivel head on kid-edged bisque shoulder plate with modeled bosom and shoulder blades, dark blue glass paperweight inset eyes, thick dark eyeliner, rose blushed eye shadow, painted lashes, brush-stroked and multi-feathered brows, accented eye corners, shaded nostrils, slightly parted richly shaded lips, tongue, kid bébé body with kid over wood upper arms, bisque forearms with separately sculpted fingers, bisque lower legs from the knees, bisque bare feet. Condition: generally excellent, back of tongue missing that allows biscuit to slide into torso metal funnel. Marks: Bru Jne 6 T (head and shoulders). Comments: Leon Casimir Bru, the "Bébé Gourmand" was first advertised by him in 1882, described as "delicieux bébé a surprise". The bébé has two hollow tin tubes or funnels in the torso into each leg through which the biscuit could be "digested" and fall through the trap door of the custom-designed shoes. Value Points: exceptionally fine condition and beauty of the very rare Bru bébé model with perfect bisque throughout and very sturdy body. The bébé was originally owned by Louise Edna Reggio, daughter of the Italian ambassador to Germany, and included with the doll are vintage photographs of Louise holding the doll, named "Dolly", garbed in original costumes which are still preserved. Also included with "Dolly" Gourmand, is an original French metal cradle with lavish fittings and various embroidered blankets, along with a lavish trousseau of more than 20 fine embroidered baby and child costumes in silks and fine woolens with hand-made lace trim, some embroidered "Dolly", along with booties, socks, rattles, mittens, and the original leather "trap-door" shoes labeled "Bru Jne Paris." $40,000/55,000

45. German Bisque Doll "Josephine", by Simon and Halbig with Extensive Couturier Trousseau and Provenance

21" (53 cm.) Bisque shoulder head, blue glass sleep eyes, painted lashes and brows, open mouth, slightly parted outlined lips, row of tiny teeth, brunette human hair, pierced ears, kid body, bisque arms to above the elbows. Condition: break and reglue on shoulders. Marks: S 10 H 740 dep. Comments: Simon and Halbig, circa 1895, a childhood doll "Josephine" of Louise Edna Reggio, daughter of the Italian ambassador to Germany; it was a family custom that each time the couturier created a new costume for Louise's mother she would also create a duplicate costume for Josephine the doll. Included with the doll are two vintage photographs depicting Louise Edna with Josephine and other of her dolls (including the Bru Gourmand, #44 of this catalog). Value Points: An outstanding and wonderfully preserved original trousseau, with family provenance and photographs, including 13 gowns, 6 hats, 11 miscellaneous skirts, capes and jackets, 10 undergarments, 2 silk and bone stays, 2 parasols, and more with meticulous and fashionable details. $3500/4500

46. German Bisque Character "Gretchen" by Kammer and Reinhardt with Outstanding Sculpting
19" (49 cm.) Bisque socket head, painted facial features, blue eyes, thick black upper eyeliner, short stroke brows, accented nostrils and eye corners, closed mouth with full lips, pouting expression, blonde mohair wig, composition and wooden ball-jointed body, antique costume. Condition: generally excellent. Marks: K*R 114 49. Comments: Kammer and Reinhardt, their model "Gretchen" from art character series, circa 1910. Value Points: outstanding quality of sculpting with deeply impressed frowning lines around the eyes and mouth, finest quality of bisque, original wig, body, body finish. $3000/4000

47. German Bisque Pouty Character, "Marie" by Kammer and Reinhardt
12" (30 cm.) Bisque socket head, painted facial features, blue eyes with decorative glaze, thick black upper eye liner, one stroke tapered brows, closed mouth with accent line between the pouty lips, blonde mohair wig with side coiled braids, composition and wooden ball-jointed body, wearing antique white cotton dress, undergarments, shoes, socks. Condition: generally excellent, some typical wig pulls at back crown rim. Marks: K*R 101 30. Comments: Kammer and Reinhardt, circa 1910, the model "Marie" from the early art reform character series. Value Points: lovely bisque, original wig, body and body finish, original costume on the petite sized doll. $1200/1800

48. Rare German Bisque Portrait Lady, 152, by Simon and Halbig with Extraordinary Expression
20" (51 cm.) Bisque socket head portraying an adult woman with slender elongated face, sculpted intaglio shaded blue eyes, heavily modeled eyelids with fringed brows, brush-stroked brows with feathered detail, aquiline nose, shaded nostrils, closed mouth, shaded and accented lips, blonde mohair wig in upswept fashion, pierced ears, composition and wooden ball-jointed body with adult female shape, elongated slender limbs, wearing antique walking suit, undergarments, bonnet, ankle boots. Condition: generally excellent. Marks: Simon & Halbig S&H 152 7 (head) Heinrich Handwerck Germany (body). Comments: Simon and Halbig, circa 1910. Value Points: the very rare portrait model in fine larger size has superb portrait expression enhanced by finest quality of sculpting, bisque and painting, original body and body finish, wig, period costume. $17,000/22,000

33

49. Extremely Rare French Bisque Artist Doll by Albert Marque with Original Body
22" (56 cm.) Bisque socket head designed with a unique four-part mold has an elongated slender face with defined temples and very full cheeks, almond-shaped blue glass inset eyes, painted curly lashes, incised eyeliner that separates the upper lashes, brush-stroked and feathered brows, accented nostrils and eye corners, rounded nose tip of curved nose, closed mouth with full lips, defined chin, prominent pierced ears, blonde mohair wig, uniquely-designed composition body with elongated torso, undefined waist, elongated composition upper arms and side-hip-jointed legs with shapely calves, small ankles, large feet, bisque lower arms with attached bisque ball-joint at the elbows, separately modeled fingers, lovely antique costume. Condition: generally excellent, very faint old curved vertical line on the throat appears original, flawless complexion, perfect original body and bisque hands. Marks: A. Marque (incised signature) #6 (red ink script). Comments: French, circa 1912. During the early 20th century during the epoch known as The Renaissance of the French Doll, the noted French sculptor Albert Marque (1872-1939) was commissioned to sculpt a doll. The doll was to depict a young girl poised on the threshold of womanhood. Her features were highly characterized, bold yet hesitant, elegant yet awkward, romantic yet realistic. The four part mold, unique in the doll industry, and with the added emphasis of hand-pressed details, allowed for this full expression. For the body design, Albert Marque enlisted the aid of a fellow artist, Aristodeme Botta; the completely unique body was produced in small cottage workshops. For the production of the head and bisque

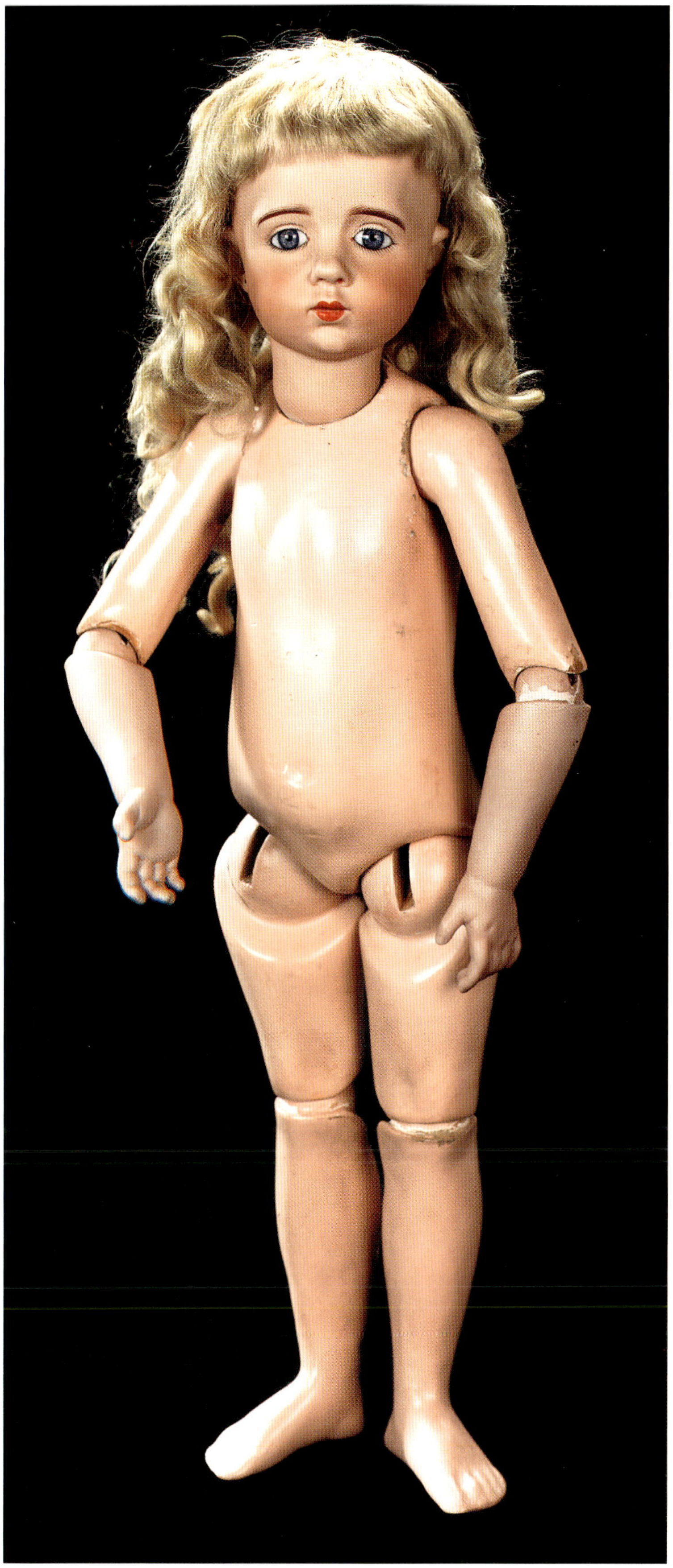

arms, Societe Francaise des Bébés et Jouets was chosen. It is believed less than 50 models of the doll were created, each numbered in red ink script, and it is probable that, at the time, a registration of these dolls was maintained in the Parisian boutique of Margaine Lacroix of Boulevard Haussman who costumed and presented the dolls to wealthy Parisians and foreign travelers. It is the only doll that Albert Marque ever created. He continued his work in bronze and terra cotta sculpture until his death in 1939, although living in great poverty. Value Points: extremely rare doll, this being #6 of the series of 50 dolls, its rarity is rivaled by its extraordinary artistry and quality of workmanship. Ex-collection Beverly Myers of Solon, Ohio until its acquisition by Geri Baker in 1993. $90,000/150,000

50. French Glazed Terra Cotta Bust "Tete de Jeune Femme" by Albert Marque

11" (28 cm.) Of textured sand-colored terra cotta with fired enhancing glaze, the bust depicts a pensive young girl whose modeling is most suggesting of the bisque doll designed by the same artist, Albert Marque. Signed A. Marque on front right shoulder. French, circa 1905, the very rare model may well be the bust presented by Marque in the 1904 Salon d'Automne, later evolved into the bisque doll he created for The Renaissance of the French Doll. Excellent condition. $3000/4000

51. Rare French Terra Cotta Bust of Young Boy by Albert Marque

17" (43 cm.) A terra cotta sculpture on self-plinth portrays a young boy with sculpted hair smoothly brushed to the side, and solemn expression. The sculpture is signed "A Marque (impressed signature script) 1930". Excellent condition. A rare model by the noted French artist, Albert Marque, 1930. $3500/5500

52. Petite French Terra Cotta Sculpture of Young Child on Marble Base by Albert Marque

6" (15 cm.) A terra cotta sculpture depicts a sad-faced child with sculpted hair drawn away from face into tousled curls at the back of her head, having downcast eyes and lips, mounted upon a green marble plinth. Singed "A. Marque" in impressed signature. Albert Marque, France, circa 1920. Excellent condition. $1000/1500

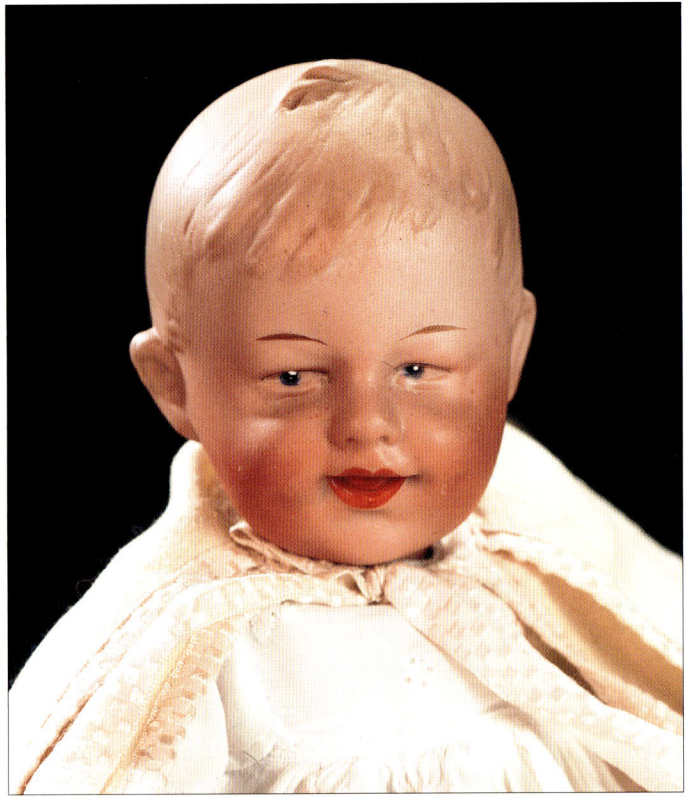

53. German Bisque Laughing Character, 7911, by Gebruder Heubach
11" (28 cm.) Solid domed bisque socket head with pink tinted bisque, sculpted short baby hair with topknot curl, squinting painted side-glancing eyes, white eye dots, one stroke brows, closed mouth with laughing expression, two beaded upper teeth, tongue, composition bent limb baby body, antique baby costume and flannel cape. Condition: generally excellent. Marks: Heubach (in square) 7911 Germany. Comments: Gebruder Heubach, circa 1912. Value Points: very appealing mischievous expression on the side-glancing character. $400/500

54. Rare German Bisque "Smiling Bye-lo" designed by Grace S. Putnam
13" (33 cm.) circ. 16"l. Solid domed bisque head with flanged neck, painted baby hair and brows, narrow blue glass eyes, painted lashes, accented nostrils, closed mouth in wide beaming smile with defined space between the outlined lips, muslin baby body with celluloid hands. Condition: generally excellent. Marks: copr. by Grace S. Putnam Germany No 15/48 (head) Bye-lo Baby...(body stamp). Comments: circa 1925, designed by Grace Putnam, designer of the Bye-lo Baby, the model closely resembles the Bye-lo with variations in eye shape and cheerful expression. Value Points: very rare character with fine quality of bisque and painting, original body, antique costume. $800/1200

55. Collection of Five German All-Bisque Kewpies
10" (25 cm.) largest. Each is all-bisque Kewpie in classic standing pose, with loop-jointed arms, starfish-shaped fingers, modeled topknot and forelock curls, right side-glancing eyes with decorative glaze, blue wings, thin line impish smile. Condition: generally excellent. Marks: O'Neill (impressed on feet) (two with original chest and back paper labels). Comments: Kewpie, circa 1912, produced in Germany. Value Points: delightful graduated size set of the Rose O'Neill characters. $800/1100

56. Extremely Rare German Bisque "Fly-Lo" Designed by Grace S. Putnam
9.5" (24 cm.) circ. 11" l. Solid domed bisque head with flanged neck has sculpted brown hair with well-defined forelock curls, blue glass sleep eyes, thick black eyeliner, ochre eye shadow encircling the eyes, tinted brows, closed mouth with well-defined lips, rosy cheeks, muslin body in the Bye-lo shape, celluloid hands, wearing factory original taffeta body suit with "wings". Condition: generally excellent, some costume dust. Marks: copr. by Grace. S. Putnam Germany. Comments: "Fly-Lo", the angel twin to the American artist Grace Putnam's popular Bye-lo Baby; the Fly-lo baby never achieved the popularity of the Bye-lo and few models are known to exist. Value Points: extremely rare model with outstanding quality of modeling and bisque, original costume, included is a matching size Bye-lo Baby partner. $2000/3000

57. 19th Century French Miniature Painting "Little Girl with Doll Picking Cherries" by Luigi Loir
4.5" (11 cm.) x 3" painting. 8" x 9" framed. A miniature gouache painting with hints of impressionistic style depicts a fashionably dressed young girl in red dress and bonnet, clasping her little doll dressed in an identical blue costume, plucking cherries from a nearby branch. The painting is signed L.L. Circa 1885. The Austrian-born French painter (1845-1916) was only 20 years of age when he first exhibited at the Salon de Paris in 1865. Scenes of life in Paris, particularly in miniature, and particularly featuring children, were his specialty for the next half-century and he was awarded medals of honor at numerous exhibitions including the 1889 Universal Exposition in Paris. Superb original condition, the painting was sold from the original atelier of the French painter Luigi Loir before its acquisition for the Baker Collection. $1000/1500

58. 19th Century French Miniature Painting "La Visite" by Luigi Loir
3" (8 cm.) x 4 1/2" painting. 7" x 9" framed. The miniature gouache painting depicts a beautifully detailed interior scene in which a fashionably dressed girl with blue bonnet is presenting her little doll, to the out-stretched arms of another well-dressed girl she is visiting. The costume details extend to minute and authentic costumes details that vary on each child, and there are beautifully rendered architectural and decorative details. The painting title "La Visite" is lettered in the left corner, and the initials L.L. are in lower right. Luigi Loir, French, circa 1885. A superb miniature painting of a tender domestic childhood scene. $1000/1500

59. Outstanding French Bisque Bébé Triste by Emile Jumeau in Superb Original Costume and Box
24" (61 cm.) Pressed bisque socket head with elongated sculpted of plump cheeks, inset blue glass paperweight eyes, dark eyeliner encircling the eye-cut, painted lashes, brush-stroked and multi-feathered brows, rose blushed eye shadow, shaded nostrils and eye corners, closed mouth, modeled space between the shaded and outlined lips, separately modeled pierced ears, blonde mohair wig over cork pate, French composition eight-loose-ball-jointed body with straight wrists and plump limbs. Condition: generally excellent. Marks: 11 (head) Jumeau Medaille d'Or Paris (body). Comments: Emile Jumeau, circa 1884. Value Points: outstanding beauty and originality of the endearing child, having original soft blonde curls, original body and body finish, wearing Jumeau couturier costume of aqua sateen with flounce back and multi-tiers of lace and pleats, bavolet bonnet, embroidered lace undergarments, blue knit stockings, leather shoes signed Bébé Jumeau, original turquoise and gilded necklace and earrings, original ivory silk and lace parasol, and in her original box. The doll is featured on the cover of *The Encyclopedia of French Dolls*. $18,000/23,000

60. Superb Earliest Period French Bisque Bébé EJ, Size 9, with Fine Antique Costume
24" (61 cm.) Pressed bisque socket head with very plump facial modeling and cheeks, blue glass paperweight inset eyes, thick dark eyeliner, painted lashes, mauve blushed eye shadow, brush-stroked and multi-feathered brows, accented eye corners, shaded nostrils, closed mouth with defined space between the outlined lips, separately modeled pierced ears, blonde mohair wig over cork pate, French composition and wooden eight-loose-ball-jointed body with straight wrists. Condition: generally excellent. Marks: 9 EJ (head) Jumeau Medaille d'Or Paris (body). Comments: Emile Jumeau, circa 1880. Value Points: rare early model in fine larger size with superior quality of sculpting, choice bisque and painting, beautifully costumed in antique lace dress with rose silk ribbons, undergarments, stockings, leather shoes signed "Bébé Jumeau Depose". $8000/11,000

61. Grand French Painting "Young Girl with Doll" by Carrier-Belleuse
56" (142 cm.) x 36". Pastel on canvas in delicate colors depicts a young girl with long brunette hair, wearing deep rose colored summer dress, seated on a chair with a doll in her lap. The doll is dressed in her original pale rose silk dress and wide ruffled bonnet. The painting is signed "Carrier Belleuse" on lower right, and the back canvas is faintly lettered "1901 C.B.". Presented under glass in a superb gilded gesso over carved wooden frame with elaborate garland. French, 1901, Louis-Robert Carrier-Belleuse, 1851-1932, the painter is listed in Benezit, studied at l'Ecole des Beaux Arts, earned a silver medal at 1889 Universal Exposition in Paris. $9000/15,000

62. Extremely Rare French Wooden Court Doll Portraying Marie Antoinette

14" (36 cm.) One piece carved wooden head and torso portraying adult woman with elaborately arranged coiffure, carved facial features, painted large blue eyes in sculpted eye sockets, arched brows, aquiline nose, closed mouth with well-shaped lips, sculpted ears, adult female modeled body with highly detailing sculpting of female elements, hinge jointed one-piece legs, painted red shoes, muslin upper arms, wooden forearms and sculpted fingers, antique silk costume with elaborate trim. Condition: generally excellent. Comments: French, circa 1780, from a series of one-of-a-kind dolls representing members of the French court of Louis XVI; this model, representing Marie-Antoinette, is documented in a landmark research work "Les Poupées Royales de la Cour de Louis XVI" by Francois Theimer; four pages are dedicated to the doll with historical photographs. Value Points: very important historical doll with outstanding detail of hair carving, the doll was previously in the important collections of Gladys Hilsdorf and Mildred Seeley before its acquisition by Geri Baker. The doll appears on the cover of *The Encyclopedia of French Dolls*. $8000/11,000

63. Unique French Wooden Court Doll, Possibly the Dauphin, Late 18th Century

10" (25 cm.) Carved wooden socket head with rounded childlike features, solid dome with tinted hair, carved and painted facial features, large blue upper glancing eyes in outlined eye sockets, arched thin-line brows, closed mouth with sculpted space between the lips, wooden torso with realistically sculpted male elements, wooden arms jointed at shoulders and elbows, one piece wooden legs with painted blue stockings and red shoes, early brocade and silk costume. Condition: very good with original painting finish with some fading, some costume frailty. Comments: circa 1780, from the very rare one-of-a-kind series of court dolls, France, represented various figures in the court of Louis XVI; according to new research by French doll historian Francois Theimer, the doll may represent the Dauphin of 1781. Value Points: very rare early carved wooden doll with documented history, owned by Mildred Seeley prior to its acquisition by Geri Baker. $4000/5000

64. 18th Century Style Wooden Doll's Bed

16" (41 cm.) The walnut bed features a high paneled back supporting a canopy roof top that is supported at the foot by two high carved pillars. The bed is fitted with linen covered frame; tapestry bed covers (not original) are included. Excellent condition. $500/800

65. Very Fine Early Wooden Room with Sculpted Ceiling and Walls

17" (43 cm.) h. x 17"l. x 13"d. A wooden framed room with ball feet and carved architectural detail at the roof line has superb detail of carved wooden ceiling with painted and gilded highlights, carved back wall featuring gilded urns, garlands and tall case clock with actual porcelain face flanked by a pair of tall mirrors. The faux-marble floor is blue and cream and their are elaborately constructed original draperies with metallic gilded edging at three sides. A gilded chandelier suspends from the ceiling and the room is furnished with a superb cast bronze ensemble with hand-painted miniature scenes in the Watteau manner, comprising unusual chaise, side chair, foot stool and three panel screen, along with bronze pedestal with metal bust. Very good condition, original front glass panel missing, some wear to paintings on furniture. Outstanding detail of decoration on the early room. Late 18th century. $4500/6500

66. An Outstanding Early Trunk with Hand-Stitched Puppet Costumes, Accessories and Script

17" (43 cm.) x 14" trunk. A wooden domed trunk with leather cover and wooden straps opens to a brimming-full collection of puppet costumes and accessories, for about 18" puppets. Each of the costumes is hand-stitched in very sturdy manner with fanciful and lavish decorative trim to represent various aristocratic and military characters of the early 19th century. Included are 16 coats, 5 dresses or capes, 3 bi-corn hats, 7 other hats to match costumes, 1 magician cap, and various accessories, viz. 8 swords, 4 rifles, 1 horsehead, 1 dragon, and 1 snake; there are 50 pieces total. Included with the collection is a hand-written theatre script "Mandrin" listing each of the "personnages" in the three-act performance. Condition: generally excellent, some age wear on fabric that is inconsequential. Comments: French, early 19th century, the set is similar to those remaining fragments at Nohant, the country home of Georges Sands, French female author of that period who is often referred to as the first Bohemian author, and who presented a remarkable theatre for her children in the garret of that home. Value Points: outstanding handmade theatre presentation pieces, carefully preserved in their original wooden trunk. $5000/7500

67. French Paper Mache Articulated Polichinelle with Throne Chair

14" (36 cm.) Heavy paste paper mache Polichinelle with sculpted definition of classic front and back humps, has swivel head and peg-jointed arms and legs, sculpted facial features and bi-corn hat, sculpted costume including ruffled collar and buttons, sculpted fancy upturned shoes. Condition: generally excellent, some typical paint fading lending a pleasing patina. Comments: maker unknown, mid-19th century, French, Polichinelle was the most popular French legendary or theatrical figure throughout the 19th century, and numerous presentations were made each year in Etrennes holiday store catalog. This mid-19th century example is shown in the book *Etrennes* by Florence Theriault. Value Points: Polichinelle in a rare hard paste model with wonderfully painted features is presented in a carved wooden throne chair with original finish. $1200/1800

68. An All-Original French Paper Mache Poupée with Superb Costume

18" (46 cm.) Solid domed paper mache shoulder head with black painted pate and modeled ears, creamy complexion with blushed cheeks and eye shadow, tiny black enamel glass eyes, painted lashes and brows, accented nostrils and eye corners, open mouth with upper and lower inset teeth, hand-stitched pink leather body with shapely torso and defined muscles, padded bosom, one piece curved arms, one piece shapely legs with gusset-jointing at hips, stitched and separated fingers, tiny feet. Condition: generally excellent. Comments: French, circa 1850. Value Points: superb original pristine condition, the pretty doll with sturdy body wears her original delicate rose silk frock with fitted drop-waist, trumpet sleeves, stiff muslin stomacher, two petticoats, pantalets, black silk slippers; the original costume is so complete as to even include the original decorative silk wrist bracelets. $2000/2500

69. Pair, Early Wax Dolls with Wooden Articulated Bodies and Original Costumes

11" (28 cm.) Depicting an adult lady and gentleman, each with poured honey wax head, sculpted hair and painted facial features, and each on original all-wooden Grodnertal-type body with dowel-jointing at shoulders, elbows, hips and knees, painted lower arms and legs, painted red flat shoes. Condition: generally excellent. Comments: Grodnertal, circa 1840. Value Points: fine details of head modeling include ringlet curls tucked behind her ears on the woman, and goatee and sideburns on gentleman; each with its original hand-sewn silk costume decorated with metallic threads or silk embroidery. $1100/1600

70. 19th Century All-Wooden Fully Articulated Figure with Sculpted Hair

13" (33 cm.) The all-wooden doll has sculpted swivel head with defined facial features and curly short hair, shapely torso with ball-swivel at the waist, elongated limbs with dowel jointing at the shoulders, elbows, wrists, hips, knees and ankles, defined toes and fingers. Condition: generally excellent. Comments: mid-19th century, the classic artist's mannequin form with extra details of facial and hair carving; the classic mannequin was the inspiration for the deposed wooden poupée body of Bru, and in this instance the face of the mannequin is highly similar to Bru's depose smiling poupée. Value Points: rare and historically important figure in doll history. $1200/1500

71. French Paper Mache Portrait of Gentleman with Handsome Visage

17" (43 cm.) One piece paper mache head and torso, slender elongated face and throat, head tilted upward in superior pose, painted facial features, blue eyes, heavily lidded eyes, aquiline closed mouth, strong chin, auburn hemp hair, pin-jointed elongated arms and legs, wearing silk Marquis costume with bicorn hat, knit stockings, black silk shoes with silver buckles. Condition: generally excellent, some fading of facial complexion. Comments: French, maker unknown, mid-19th century. Value Points: very handsome features of gentleman with portrait like qualities. $2000/3000

72. German Porcelain Taufling Baby with Loosely Jointed Limbs

11" (28 cm.) Solid domed porcelain swivel head on porcelain shoulder plate, black painted baby hair, sculpted ears, painted facial features, blue eyes, red and black upper eyeliner, closed mouth with hint of impish smile, porcelain lower torso and lower arms and legs, bare feet, muslin midriff and upper arms and legs. Condition: restoration to shoulder plate and hidden neck rim of head, otherwise excellent. Comments: circa 1860, considered the historically first model of the classic child doll with jointed limbs that came into popularity some two decades earlier. Value Points: very rare doll especially as swivel head model, has all original parts, bare feet, great expression. $1200/1700

73. Early German Porcelain Taufling Baby with Porcelain Lower Limbs

11" (28 cm.) Porcelain swivel head with flat-cut neck on porcelain shoulder plate, solid dome, painted black baby hair, sculpted ears, painted blue eyes, red and black upper eyeliner, single stroke brows, accented nostril dots, closed mouth, porcelain hips and lower arms and legs, muslin midriff and upper limbs, antique baby dress. Condition: fine professional restoration to back shoulder plate and arms, otherwise all parts are excellent and original. Comments: Germany, circa 1860, the doll was inspired by the Japanese Ichimatsu doll with loosely-jointed limbs introduced at the mid-19th century London International Exposition, and was the forerunner of the later French and German child doll. Value Points: very rare model with original body, great facial expression. $1200/1700

74. Petite German Porcelain Grey-Haired Lady by KPM

9" (23 cm.) Pink tinted porcelain shoulder head with oval shaped face and elongated throat, sculpted short curls of grey/taupe with fine detail of stippling, painted facial features, muslin body, porcelain lower limbs, wearing antique lace dress over rose silk lining, undergarments. Condition: generally excellent. Marks: (KPM crossed swords). Comments: circa 1880. Value Points: rare petite model with exquisite minute detail of hair painting, rich creamy complexion. $700/1000

74.

75.

76.

75. German Porcelain Dollhouse Lady with Wooden Articulated Body
7" (18 cm.) Porcelain shoulder head with delicate pink tinted complexion, black sculpted hair in soft finger curls, painted facial features, on wooden articulated body with shapely torso, dowel-jointing at shoulders elbows, hips and knees, porcelain lower arms and legs, painted red flat shoes. Condition: generally excellent, left arm is not original. Comments: Germany, circa 1860. Value Points: rare wooden body, along with original early gown and pantalets. $800/1200

76. Early German Porcelain Lady with Brown Hair by KPM
14" (36 cm.) Porcelain shoulder head depicting adult lady with slender oval face and very elongated strong throat with defined hollow, light pink tinted complexion, brown sculpted hair in center part waved smoothly around the face with four ringlet curls at each ear and a coiled chignon at the back, painted blue down-glancing heavily lidded eyes with red liner, aquiline nose, closedmouth, muslin stitch-jointed body with stitched-on stocking and shoes, leather arms, lovely antique costume. Condition: generally excellent. Marks: KPM (red and blue stamps inside shoulder plate). Comments: KPM, Germany, circa 1845. Value Points: very rare early porcelain lady with brown hair, superb sculpting and painting. $3000/4000

77. Very Rare Large German Porcelain Lady with Wooden Articulated Body
19" (48 cm.) Thick paste porcelain shoulder plate depicting an adult woman with slender oval face, elongated throat, slightly modeled bosom, sculpted black hair in long ringlet curls with comb-marked details, painted blue eyes in deeply set sockets, black and red upper eyeliner, single stroke brows, aquiline nose with accented nostrils, closed mouth with center accent line, wooden body with slender shaped torso, dowel-jointing at shoulders, elbows, hips and knees, porcelain lower arms and legs, painted orange shoes. Condition: generally excellent, one ankle reglued. Comments: Germany, circa 1850. Value Points: very beautiful porcelain lady doll with refined features, outstanding sculpting, rare wooden body with porcelain limbs in larger size. $4500/5500

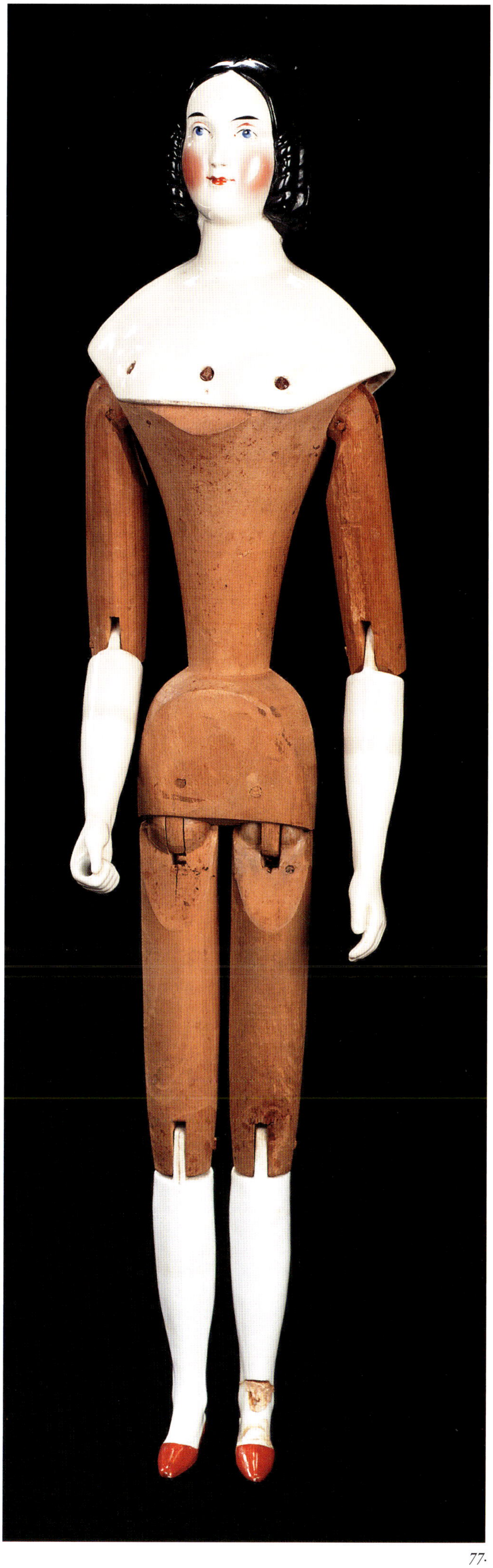

77.

unusual costume suggest the doll may have been presented to represent the French author, Georges Sands, a notable subject of stylized portraiture throughout the 19th century. Value Points: the outstanding portrait doll with highly refined aristocratic features is enhanced by her all original and most unique hunting ensemble of green velvet with brown felt fedora, and carrying finely crafted leather accessories including collar, supply strap, gaiters, and belt, along with finely woven pouch and walnut-cased faux-rifle with cast mountings. $5000/7500

79. Early French Bisque Porcelain Poupée with Bisque Arms

14" (36 cm.) Bisque swivel head on kid-edged bisque shoulder plate, plump facial modeling, cobalt blue glass enamel inset eyes, dark eyeliner, painted lashes and brows, closed mouth with accent line between the lips, ears pierced into head, kid body with gusset jointing at hips and knees, kid over wooden upper arms, bisque lower arms with dowel jointed elbows, curled fingers. Condition: generally excellent. Comments: circa 1860 in the Barrois manner. Value Points: beautiful pale bisque complements the brilliant eyes, bisque arms, original elaborate coiffure, fine antique costume. $3000/4000

80. French Bisque Poupée with Rare Dehors Signature and Deposed Dehors Articulation

14" (36 cm.) Pale bisque swivel head on bisque shoulder plate, neck articulation system allowing the head to tilt forward and side to side in addition to the standard swivel, cobalt blue glass enamel inset eyes, painted lashes, lightly feathered brows, accented nostrils, closed mouth with pale accented lips, unpierced ears, brunette human hair over cork pate, kid poupée body with very shapely torso, gusset-jointing at hips and knees, kid-over-wooden upper arms, bisque arms to above the elbows. Condition: generally excellent, tip of one index finger chipped. Marks: A. Dehors (incised) Comments: Alexandre Dehors who deposed the unique neck articulation in 1866, allowing the poupée to tilt head "modestly or triumphantly" according to depose description. Value Points: few examples of signed poupées by Dehors are known to exist, this example has delicate beauty and lovely pale complexion, rarer bisque arms, Dehors deposed neck articulation, wearing early white pique gown with soutache trim, undergarments, leather ankle boots, bonnet; an additional gown is included; the doll was acquired by Geri Baker from "A Fully Perfected Grace", #154, (see for further photographs). $3500/4500

78. Superb French Bisque Portrait Poupée in Original Hunting Costume with Accessories

16" (41 cm.) Pressed bisque swivel head on kid-edged shoulder plate, very elongated slender face with pale complexion, strong modeling of aquiline nose, chin line and cheek bones, blue glass enamel inset eyes, painted lashes and brows, accented nostrils, closed mouth with accent line between the pale lips, brunette mohair wig over cork pate, kid gusset-jointed poupée body, Condition: generally excellent. Comments: French, circa 1865, the strong facial lines and

81. Exceptionally Rare French Bisque Poupée by Dehors with Portrait Face 18" (46 cm.) Pale bisque swivel head on bisque shoulder plate with distinctly modeled bosom, unique hidden system of neck articulation allowing the head to tilt side to side and forward as well as classic swivel, oval-shaped elongated face with aquiline-shaped nose, heavily-lidded blue glass enamel inset eyes, painted lashes and brows, closed mouth with accented lips and hint of smile, pierced ears, blonde mohair wig over cork pate, kid poupée body with shapely torso, gusset-jointed legs, wood articulated arms with jointing at shoulders, elbows, and wrists. Condition: generally excellent. Comments: Alexander Dehors, his brevete model of 1866, created for presentation at the 1867 Paris International Exposition and designed to compete against the Huret style poupée; in fact, the Exposition jury declared the unique neck articulation of the Dehors doll was "an extra not found in Huret dolls". Value Points: rare deposed history model with superb portrait face, wonderful early (frail) fashion gown and accessories including minature Borzoi dog. $7000/9000

82. Very Rare French Bisque Bébé Brevete, Size 6/0, by Leon Casimir Bru with Signed Shoes and Bonnet

11" (28 cm.) Pressed bisque swivel head on kid-edged bisque shoulder plate, very plump cheeks and chin, pale complexion with softly blushed cheeks and chin, blue glass enamel inset eyes, painted lashes and brows, dark eyeliner, accented nostrils of rounded nose, closed mouth with accented lips, pierced ears, blonde mohair wig over cork pate, French kid gusset-jointed bébé body, bisque lower arms, wearing early maroon silk dress with lace trim, undergarments, stockings, leather shoes, bonnet. Condition: generally excellent. Marks: 6/0 (head and shoulder plate). Comments: Leon Casmir Bru, circa 1878, his first model of bébé. Value Points: very rare earliest model Bru bébé has outstanding bisque, sculpting and painting, original body based upon Bru depose with bisque lower arms, signed "B" shoes and original Bru label inside bonnet. $12,000/15,000

83. An Outstanding French Bisque Bébé A.T. by Thuillier with Signed A.T. Shoes

18" (46 cm.) Pressed bisque swivel head on kid-edged bisque shoulder plate, sculpted features include rounded pointy nose tip and chin, full cheeks, heavy-lidded blue glass paperweight inset eyes with large black pupils, thick black eyeliner, painted lashes, mauve blushed eye shadow, brush-stroked feathered brows, accented eye corners, shaded nostrils, closed mouth with shaded and outlined lips, heart-shaped upper lip, pierced ears, blonde mohair wig over cork pate, French kid bébé body with square cut collarette, gusset-jointing at elbows, hips and knees, bisque forearms with separately sculpted fingers, defined knuckles and nails. Condition: generally excellent, some kid patching on original body. Marks: A. 7 T. (head and shoulder plate). Comments: Andre Thuillier, circa 1880, his first period bébé. Value Points: outstanding beauty of the very rare early bébé whose quality of bisque and sculpting is enhanced further by artful painting, antique wig, original body with beautifully sculpted hands, wonderful antique ivory silk costume and bonnet, leather shoes signed A.T. The doll was acquired by Geri Baker from the Mildred Seeley Collection and is featured in *The Encyclopedia of French Dolls*, page 620.
$35,000/45,000

84. Pair, German Miniature Bisque Dolls in Original Soldier Costumes
5" (13 cm.) Each has bisque socket head, painted facial features, blue eyes, single stroke brows, closed mouth, blonde mohair wig, five piece paper mache body with painted boots. Condition: generally excellent. Marks: 13/0. Comments: Germany, circa 1890. Value Points: the pair of little soldiers are wearing their original school boy military costumes with matching jackets, short pants, caps, and toy swords, acquired by Geri Baker from the Legoland Antique Toy Museum Collection. $500/800

85. Outstanding French Bisque Bébé by Leon Casimir Bru, Size 11, with Signed Shoes
28" (71 cm.) Pressed bisque swivel head on kid-edged bisque shoulder plate with modeled bosom and shoulder blades, blue glass paperweight inset eyes of great depth, thick dark eyeliner, painted curly lashes, rose blushed eye shadow, brush-stroked and multi-feathered brows, accented eye corners, shaded nostrils, closed mouth with shaded and outlined lips, dimpled chin and lip corners, pierced ears, blonde mohair wig over cork pate, kid bébé body with slender torso, kid over wooden upper arms, bisque forearms, Chevrot hinged upper kid over wooden legs, wooden lower legs, beautifully costumed in vintage dress of antique silks and velvets, undergarments, bonnet, leather shoes signed Bru Jne Paris. Condition: generally excellent, one finger reglued. Marks: Bru Jne 11 (head and shoulders) (original Bru paper label on chest). Comments: Leon Casimir Bru, circa 1885. Value Points: outstanding example of the classic era Bru bébé in grand size with exemplary bisque and painting, luminous eyes, original body in choice condition. $25,000/30,000

86. French Velvet Vitrine with Curved Glass Front
7" (18 cm.) The wooden-framed table-top vitrine is covered with rich burgundy red velvet and overlaid with an ormolu border of vines and berries with garland crest at the front centered by two finials. The curved glass front opens to a tufted silk cushion and mirrored back. Excellent condition. French, circa 1880. $700/1000

87. Superb Regency Miniature Chest with Lion's Head Bronze Hardware
16" (41 cm.) l. 13"h. Of fine fruitwood with burled walnut veneers, the Regency style chest features a single drawer above two-door cabinet, having marble top and luxury cast bronze fittings and medallions including a pair of lion heads on the cabinet doors. Excellent condition. Circa 1820. $800/1200

88. German Bisque Pouting Character, 7759, by Gebruder Heubach

14" (36 cm.) Solid domed bisque socket head, blonde painted short boyish hair with comb-marked detail, intaglio tiny blue eyes with black upper eyeliner, tiny white eye dots, short stroke brows, accented nostrils, closed mouth with downcast lips, composition and wooden ball-jointed body, wearing antique lined dress with embroidered trim, cap, undergarments, shoes and red knit stockings. Condition: generally excellent. Marks: Heubach (square) 5 7759. Comments: Gebruder Heubach, circa 1912. Value Points: rarer model with appealing shy and wistful expression, original body and body finish. $900/1200

89. Rare German Bisque Character by Bahr and Proschild for Swaine & Co

14" (36 cm.) Bisque socket head, intaglio narrow blue eyes with tiny white eye dots, black upper eyeliner, impressed laughter crinkles, short feathered brows, closed mouth in shy smile with outlined lips and row of beaded teeth, blonde mohair fleecy wig, original composition body with shoulder and hip jointing, painted knee-high stockings and black ankle-strap shoes, wearing original school dress, undergarments and cap. Condition: generally excellent. Marks: B.P. 5 (incised) Geschutz Germany S&C (green stamp). Comments: Bahr and Proschild for Swaine, circa 1915. Value Points: rare model with most endearing expression of cheerful yet shy child, wonderful detail of sculpting, original rarer body. $2000/3000

90. German Wooden Toy Horse and Carriage

11" (28 cm.) A creamy hide-covered wooden horse with brown glass eyes and elaborate leather harness has tiny hidden wheeled feet, and is attached to a two-wheeled wooden cart with silk tufted seat and carpeted floor. Excellent condition. Circa 1890. $400/500

91. Wonderful 19th Century Double Team of Horses on Wooden Platform
24" (61 cm.) h. 26. l. A wooden platform with four cast iron spoked wheels supports a matched pair of black and white spotted hide over wooden ponies, posed in prancing pose, with horsehair mane and tail, glass eyes, elaborate leather harness and saddle. Excellent condition. Circa 1880, rare double team in larger size with wonderful pose, original leather work. $900/1400

92. Large German Bisque Toddler "Erika" by Simon and Halbig
26" (66 cm.) Bisque socket head with rounded facial shape, small blue glass sleep eyes, dark eyeliner, painted curly lashes, short brush-stroked brows with feathered details, accented nostrils of upturned nose, open mouth, outlined lips, row of porcelain teeth, brunette mohair wig, composition and wooden ball-jointed toddler body with side-hip jointing, antique cotton school dress, bonnet, undergarments, shoes, stockings. Condition: generally excellent. Marks: 1489 Erika Simon & Halbig 14. Comments: Simon and Halbig, circa 1912. Value Points: rare model with unusual and most appealing facial expression, enhanced by finest quality bisque and painting, rarer toddler body with original finish. $3000/4000

93. *Early English Faux-Stone Doll House with Eight Fireplaces*
42" (107 cm.) chimney to floor. 36"w. 24" d. Elaborately-gabled English-style house has exterior of faux-stone facade in rich detail, high peak twin gable roof with shake shingles, three chimneys, paneled front door with fan glass window, small front porch with arched crest decorated with a deer's head founder's plate, double columns, two large bay windows, one small oriel window on each side, 15 windows total. The interior contains double attic with outside hinged access from two sides, 8 rooms on two additional floors, plus central hallway, foyer and staircase. Each room has a different fireplace with mantel of lithographed or elaborate hand-painted details to simulate tile, brick or other materials, and brass or painted cornices. The main central staircase has a lithographed carpet runner; an ornately carved railing encircles the stairwell at the second floor landing. Interior door to all rooms lead from the center hallway, and the pantry/kitchen has light fixture and metal sink. Very good condition, one piece of outside trim missing, some interior wall and floor papers scraped. English, mid-19th century. $8000/11,000

94. Large American Wooden Doll House with Mansard Roof

61" (155 cm.) h. with chimney, 44"d., 22" w. The large wooden doll house has a full-width front panel that hinges open with bottom wheel to reveal three floors with seven rooms (including basement room) There are four side windows, 15 front windows and 2 chimneys. There is a detachable front roof with 5 windows that removes to reveal 3 attic rooms. The front door opens into the center staircase and there are hinged doors that open into the rooms on 1st and 2nd floors. The first floor living room has fireplace. The exterior finish which appears original is red with black trim, with a black Mansard-shaped roof. The interior painted rooms include bottom left kitchen covered with old lithographs mostly children at play. Very good as found condition. American, New York Brownstone style, circa 1885. $6000/9000

95. German Cloth Character "Max-Martin" in Leiderhausen by Kathe Kruse
17" (43 cm.) All cloth doll with plump facial modeling, pressed and oil painted face, brown painted eyes, black upper eyeliner, thick brown eye shadow, closed mouth, shaded lips, brunette mohair side-parted wig, stitch-jointed shoulders, hip-jointed legs. Condition: generally excellent. Marks: 921902 (foot) KK Unique Art Doll (original paper label on wrist) (and other paper label Made in US Zone KK with ink lettered name "Max-Martin IM/38". Comments: Kathe Kruse, circa 1945. Value Points: fine original lustrous complexion on the wigged model doll, wearing original brown felt flannel leiderhausen and Tyrolean hat with felt flowers. $1200/1700

96. German Cloth Character "Dick" by Kathe Kruse
17" (43 cm.) All cloth doll with pressed and oil-painted face and hair, short brown hair with stippled curls onto the forehead, brown painted eyes, black and brown upper eyeliner, accented nostrils, closed mouth with pouting expression, shaded ears, stitch-jointed shoulders, disc-jointed legs. Condition: generally excellent. Marks: 720640 (foot stamp) Kathe Kruse (original paper label with ink lettered name "Dick"). Comments: Kathe Kruse, circa 1930s. Value Points: artful painting of the sad-featured boy wearing original costume, with two original paper labels. $1200/1700

97. German Cloth Character Girl in Red Flowered Dress
17" (43 cm.) All cloth doll with rounded facial shape, oil painted face and hair, short swirled curls, brown shaded eyes, black upper eyeliner, brown eye shadow, accented nostrils, closed mouth, stitch-jointing at shoulders, disc-jointed legs. Condition: generally excellent. Marks: 120436 (foot). Kathe Kruse Made in US Zone Germany (paper label). Comments: Kathe Kruse, circa 1945. Value

Points: beautifully preserved original painted features of wistful child, wearing original flowered dress, pinafore, undergarments, stockings, shoes, cap, original paper label. $1100/1500

98. German Wooden Doll House by Moritz Gottschalk
34" (86 cm.) h. x 30"w. x 14"d. The wooden two story doll house with original yellow painted exterior with red room and white trim, opens at the front in two sections to reveal four rooms plus attic, small toilet room by the front hall staircase, and a mini storage room at the top of the stairs. There are two exterior chimneys, railings, flower boxes, green painted front door with classic Gottshalk silver knob, staircase, attic porch, overhang on attic porch and front door entrance, The interior rooms are covered in old paper, which is partially original. Good condition, missing attic porch door and some lattice trim. The house is pencil lettered on underside "360 s". Gottschalk, circa 1910. $4000/5000

99. Large German Bisque Laughing Character, 116/A by Kammer and Reinhardt
24" (61 cm.) Bisque socket head, blue glass sleep eyes, thick dark eyeliner, painted curly lashes, brush-stroked and feathered brows, accented eye corners and nostrils, open mouth, shaded and outlined lips, tongue, two beaded upper teeth, blonde mohair wig, composition bent limb baby body, wearing antique green woolen baby coat with capelet collars, booties. Condition: generally excellent. Marks: K*R Simon & Halbig 116/A 62. Comments: Kammer and Reinhardt, circa 1912. Value Points: exceptional quality of sculpting with well defined laughter lines around the eyes and mouth, enhanced by finest bisque and painting, original wig, body, body finish. $1500/2000

100. American Composition "Ferdinand the Bull"
9" (23 cm.) All composition comic film character of the lovable side-glancing bull named Ferdinand, has swivel head and jointed legs, painted facial features with dreamy-eyed side-glancing expression, original hole in mouth for holding a flower, rope tail. Condition: generally excellent, some typical paint rubs around left eye and leg joints. Comments: circa 1940. Value Points: endearing character is hard to find. $300/400

101. German All-Bisque Doll in Original Scottish Costume, with Jointed Leg Dog
4" (10 cm.) Bisque swivel head on kid-edged bisque torso, blue glass eyes, painted lashes and brows, closed mouth, blonde mohair wig, peg-jointed bisque arms and legs, painted shoes and stockings. Condition: generally excellent. Marks: 4. Comments: Germany, circa 1890. Value Points: the little doll wears original well-detailed Scottish costume, and owns an all-bisque dog with pin-jointed bisque limbs. $400/600

102. German All-Bisque Miniature Doll with Rocking Horse
6" (15 cm.) Solid domed bisque swivel head, blue glass inset eyes, painted lashes and brows, accented nostrils, closed mouth

with pouty expression on the accented lips, blonde mohair wig, bisque peg-jointed limbs, painted stockings with blue rims, black one-strap shoes, wearing antique knit suit. Condition: generally excellent, tiny chip at neck of back torso. Marks: 2. Comments: Germany, circa 1885. Value Points: included with the swivel head pouty boy is a paper mache toy rocking horse with leather saddle. $500/700

103. Rare German Bisque Character, 1488, by Simon and Halbig
18" (46 cm.) Bisque socket head, small blue glass sleep eyes, painted curly lashes, short feathered brows with fly-away detail, accented nostrils, closed mouth with defined space between the shaded and outlined lips, blonde mohair bobbed wig, composition bent limb baby body, antique costume including romper suit, knit shoes, wool coat with brass buttons, wool cap with anchor. Condition: generally excellent. Marks: 1488 Simon & Halbig 12. Comments: Simon and Halbig, circa 1912. Value Points: rare pouting character with outstanding detail of facial modeling including defined creases around the eyes and mouth, impressed philtrum dimple, finest quality of bisque, original wig, body, body finish. $3500/4500

104. Wonderful German Bisque Character, 1498, with Sculpted Hair
12" (30 cm.) Solid domed bisque socket head, painted blonde boyish hair with decorative glaze, small blue glass sleep eyes, painted lashes and brows, accented nostrils, closed mouth with accented lips, composition and wooden ball-jointed toddler body with side-hip jointing. Condition: generally excellent. Comments: 1498 3. Comments: Simon and Halbig, circa 1912. Value Points: wonderfully expressive wistful features enhanced by fine bisque, rare painted hair, toddler body, antique velvet boy's sailor costume, rare size. $2500/3500

105. Petite German Bisque Character, 185, with Glass Eyes by Kestner
12" (30 cm.) Bisque socket head, tiny blue glass sleep eyes, painted lashes, dark eyeliner, brushstroked brows, accented nostrils and eye corners, closed mouth with row of tiny painted teeth between the smiling lips, brunette mohair wig, composition and wooden ball-jointed body. Condition: generally excellent. Marks: 185. Comments: Kestner, circa 1910. Value Points: wonderful pristine condition of the rare little girl, with original wig, body, body finish, beautiful bisque and expression, original costume, and another original silk dress, coat, and undergarments included. $2000/3000

106. German Embossed Tin Doll Carriage with All-Bisque Doll
6" (15 cm.) carriage. Pressed tin doll carriage with embossed designs to simulate wicker is constructed in rare-to-find late 19th century "high" style, having four spoked wheels with larger wheels in rear, curved metal handle, and is fitted with silk and lace blankets and contains an all-bisque miniature doll with jointed limbs, swivel head, painted features, antique costume. Excellent condition. Germany, circa 1890. $600/900

107. French All-Bisque Miniature in Original Nanny Costume
4" (10 cm.) Bisque swivel head on kid-edged bisque torso, cobalt blue glass inset eyes, painted lashes and brows, accented nostrils, closed mouth with piquant smile, original blonde mohair wig, peg-jointed bisque arms and legs, painted white stockings and two lace shoes. Condition: generally excellent. Marks: 4. Comments: Germany, circa 1890. Value Points: the all-original little doll wears her original nanny costume including gown, cape and coiffe. $400/600

108. Outstanding German Bisque Lady with Smile, Model 1388, by Simon and Halbig
22" (56 cm.) Bisque socket head, blue/grey glass inset eyes, thick black eyeliner, painted curly lashes, incised eyeliner, short feathered brows with slightly modeled effect, accented eye corners and nostrils, closed mouth with slightly upturned lip corners as though smiling, row of painted teeth, pierced ears, original brunette mohair wig, composition and wooden ball-jointed lady body with shapely torso, elongated limbs, wearing lovely sheer summer dress with printed flowers, undergarments, shoes, stockings, straw bonnet. Condition: generally excellent. Marks: 1388 Germany Simon and Halbig S&H 8 (head) Heinrich Handwerck Germany 8 1/2 (body). Comments: Simon and Halbig, circa 1900. Value Points: outstanding quality of sculpting includes impressed cheek dimples, defined laughter creases at eye and lip corners, finest quality of bisque, original body and body finish, wig, fine larger size of the rare model. $18,000/25,000

109. German Painted Metal Doll Carriage by Maerklin
9" (23 cm.) Of tin metal, the carriage has square sides and bed with gracefully curved front and is painted in shades of pale pink and cream with gilded scrolls. The carriage rests upon double spoked wheels, has fabric folding sunshade, gilded curved handles and cream wooden hand grip. Excellent condition. Original finish and shade. Maerklin, Germany, circa 1890. $1200/1800

110. German Painted Metal Doll Carriage by Maerklin
8" (20 cm.) The tin metal sleigh style doll carriage is painted pink and cream with outlined exterior panels, pink spoked wheels, gilded curved handles with black wooden hand grip, and has a folding (worn) fabric shade. Excellent condition, original finish and shade. Maerklin, Germany, circa 1890. $1200/1800

111. German All-Bisque Miniature Doll by Kestner with Yellow Boots
6" (15 cm.) Pale bisque swivel head, brown glass eyes, painted long dark lashes, thick brush stroked brows, accented nostrils, closed mouth with pert smile, blonde mohair braids, peg-jointed bisque arms and legs, painted yellow heeled boots, antique costume. Condition: generally excellent. Marks: 208 6. Comments: Kestner, circa 1910. Value Points: pretty child with beautiful pale bisque, fancy yellow boots. $400/700

112. German All-Bisque Miniature Doll with Blue Boots by Kestner
6" (15 cm.) Bisque swivel head on kid-edged bisque torso, brown glass sleep eyes, painted lashes and brows, accented nostrils, closed mouth with downcast pouty lips, blonde mohair wig, peg-jointed bisque arms and legs with shapely detail, defined knees, painted blue heeled ankle boots, white stockings with pink ribbons, wearing original rose silk and lace dress, undergarments, bonnet. Condition: generally excellent, two tiny chips at joints. Marks: 0. Comments: Kestner, circa 1885. Value Points: wonderful sweet yet sad expression on the rare early doll, blue boots. $900/1400

113. Petite German All-Bisque Miniature with Swivel Head
6" (15 cm.) Bisque swivel head brown glass inset eyes, painted lashes and brows, accented nostrils, closed mouth with outlined lips, blonde mohair wig, peg-jointed arms and legs, painted white stockings to mid-thigh, black ankle boots, wearing silk knit dress. Condition: generally excellent. Marks: 3/22 14. Comments: circa 1910. Value Points: swivel head, closed mouth, rare stockings. $400/500

114. German Bisque Child by Kammer and Reinhardt in Fine Antique Silk Jester Costume
39" (100 cm.) Bisque socket head, brown glass sleep eyes, dark eyeliner, painted lashes, brush-stroked and feathered brows with decorative glaze, accented nostrils and eye corners, open mouth, outlined lips, four porcelain teeth, pierced ears, brunette human hair wig, composition and wooden ball-jointed body. Condition: generally excellent. Marks: K*R Simon & Halbig 100. Comments: Kammer and Reinhardt, circa 1910. Value Points: wonderful large size child with gentle expression, fine bisque and painting, original body and body finish, wearing superb antique silk rose and ivory jester costume with gold braid and lace trim, gold buttons, with matching cap. $2500/3500

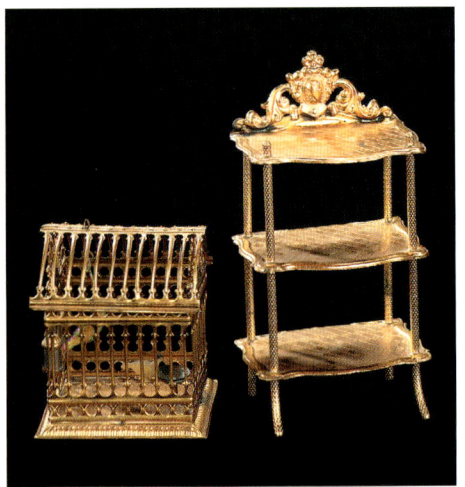

115. 19th Century Miniature Gilded Ormolu Fireplace and Mantel
6" (15 cm.) Of metal with fretwork and embossed detailing, the fireplace features a fronthearth guard with richly spindled detail, and two shelved etagere with mirrored back and elaborate scrolls and garland trim. Circa 1880. Excellent condition. $600/900

116. 19th Century Miniature Gilded Metal and Ormolu Lady's Desk
4.5" (11 cm.) The metal desk has rich sculpted detail of the writing surface and draw fronts, and an elaborately carved back. The desk rests upon boldly curved cabriole style legs with embossed reptilian design, and there are three opening drawers. Excellent condition. Circa 1880. $700/1000

117. 19th Century Miniature Ormolu Birdcage and Etagere
6" (15 cm.) etagere. Comprising a gilded metal large double birdcage in gazebo style with fancily turned spindles and frame, two water feeders, interior perch, bird bath and two birds; and three shelved etagere with curved shelves, and a fancily carved crest. Excellent condition. Circa 1880. $800/1200

118. Gilded Ormolu Miniature Mirror with Framed Lithographs
Comprising a gilded metal framed mirror in hinged brackets with ormolu base and a wide and very fancifully carved frame supporting two candle sticks. Along with two framed lithographs depicting a courtly couple, each in elaborate ormolu frame. Excellent condition. Circa 1880. $500/800

119. 19th Century Miniature Ormolu Folding Mirror and Two Candlestick Holders
3" (8 cm.) mirror. An elaborately framed ormolu gilded frame with back support, designed for use on toilette table, has lithograph prints on two exterior walls with romanticized views of boys and girls, and hinges open to reveal a triptych mirror; along with a pair of candle stick holders with leaf-shaped feet and finger holds. Circa 1880. Excellent condition. $500/900

120. 19th Century Lady's Toilette Table with Mirror
5" (13 cm.) The richly embossed dainty dressing table whose details include beaded edging, checkerboard pattern on flat surfaces, acanthus detail on the cabriole legs, and very elaborate crown on mirror, offers a pull-out jewelry drawer. Excellent condition. Circa 1880. $500/800

121. Fine 19th Century Salon Tea Table with Fitted Porcelain de Paris Service
10" (25 cm.) h. Proportioned for display with poupée or bébé, the ebony-finished wooden pedestal table with four arched legs has gilded striping and applique decoupage along the edge and on the lid; the turtle-shaped top hinges open to reveal rose paper lined interior and a fitted ribbon-tied miniature tea service of white Porcelain de Paris with blue and gilded borders and floral garlands, comprising lidded teapot, lidded sugar, creamer,

six cups and saucers, six gold-plated spoons, and a gold-plated sugar tong. Excellent condition. A very rare style miniature furniture in superb original condition. French, circa 1865. $2500/3500

122. *French Bisque Poupée by Emile Jumeau in Grand Size*
25" (64 cm.) Pressed bisque swivel head on kid-edged bisque shoulder plate, brown glass paperweight inset eyes with spiral threading, thick black eyeliner, painted lashes, rose blushed eye shadow, brush-stroked brows with decorative glaze, accented nostrils, shaded eye corners, closed mouth with outlined lips, impressed lip corners, pierced ears, blonde mohair wig over cork pate, French kid poupée body with shapely torso, gusset-jointing at elbows, hips and knees, wearing antique rose silk gown. Condition: generally excellent, some body scrub. Comments: Emile Jumeau, circa 1878. Value Points: lovely bisque on the brown-eyed poupée in grand size. $3500/4500

123. Fine French Early Model Poupée by Leon Casimir Bru with Trunk and Trousseau
15" (38 cm.) Pale bisque swivel head on kid-edged bisque shoulder plate, cobalt blue glass enamel inset eyes, thick black eyeliner, painted curly lashes, arched brows, accented nostrils and eye corners, closed mouth with outlined lips, ears pierced into head, blonde mohair wig over cork pate, kid poupée body with gusset jointing, padded bosom with square cut collarette, wooden arms with dowel-jointing at shoulders, elbows and wrists, separately carved fingers. Condition: generally excellent. Marks: D (backwards on head). Comments: Leon Casimir Bru, his signature poupée body and earliest version of the smiling poupée, circa 1865. Value Points: pristine condition of the virtually unplayed with poupée, along with her trunk and trousseau comprising three dresses, various undergarments, cape, jacket, two tabliers, fur muff in box, two hankies monogrammed "M", two fancy bonnets, white cap, corset, three pairs of ankle boots, black veil pagoda-shaped parasol with blue silk and Alencon lace cover, red leather purse with gilded chain, and a pearl jewelry arrangement in original box comprising necklace, two bracelets, watch with brooch fob, and earrings. $5000/7500

124. Grand French Bisque Bébé A.T., Size 15, by Thuillier
26" (66 cm.) Pressed bisque socket head with elongated facial modeling and very plump cheeks, almond shaped dark blue glass paperweight inset eyes, thick dark eyeliner, painted curly lashes, thick brush-stroked brows with enhancing decorative glaze and feathered highlights, accented eye corners, shaded nostrils, closed mouth with defined space between the shaded and outlined lips, pierced ears, blonde mohair wig over cork pate, French composition and wooden fully-jointed body with straight wrists, lovely antique lace costume, coat, jacket, undergarments, knit stockings, shoes. Condition: generally excellent, torso slightly dented but body is all original with original finish. Marks: A. 15 T. Comments: Thuillier, circa 1884. Value Points: especially beautiful bisque and painting with superb sculpting of mouth and lower lace, original body and body finish, fine grand size. $30,000/40,000

125. Rare Large Size French Bisque Poupée Attributed to Dehors with Deposed Articulation

35" (89 cm.) Pale bisque swivel head on kid-edged bisque shoulder plate, plump facial modeling, articulation of head that allows it to tilt side to side and forward as well as swivel, almond shaped blue glass enamel inset eyes, thick dark eyeliner, painted lashes, mauve blushed eye shadow, brushstroked brows, accented nostrils and eye corners, closed mouth with outlined lips, pierced ears, blonde mohair wig over cork pate, French kid poupée body with shapely torso, gusset-jointing at hips, knees, and elbows, stitched and separated fingers, wearing deluxe silk taffeta gown with lavish lace and floral trim, undergarments, shoes. Condition: generally excellent, some body patching. Comments: attributed to Dehors, the realistic system of neck articulation was deposed by him in 1867. Value Points: perhaps the largest model known to exist with the rare Dehors deposed articulation, enhanced by beautiful bisque and expression. $4500/6500

126. French All-Bisque Mignonette with Swivel Head

5" (13 cm.) Solid domed bisque swivel head on kid-edged bisque torso, cobalt blue glass enamel inset eyes, painted

lashes, feathered brows, accented nostrils, closed mouth, blonde mohair wig, peg-jointed bisque arms and legs, painted white stockings and brown two strap shoes, antique costume. Condition: generally excellent. Comments: French, circa 1882. Value Points: endearing facial expression, swivel head. $800/1000

127. Fine All-Original English Poured Wax Child Doll in Rare Child's Costume with Original Box
18" (46 cm.) Poured wax shoulder head with pink tinted complexion, cobalt blue glass enamel inset eyes with heavily modeled eyelids, tinted brows and eye liner, accented nostrils and eye corners, closed mouth with downcast pale lips, separately inserted delicate hair with center part, softly stuffed muslin body, wax lower limbs with bare feet. Condition: generally excellent. Comments: circa 1865. Value Points: the exquisitely preserved doll with beautiful rosy complexion wears her original ice blue silk taffeta child's dress of the 1860 era, with undergarments, leather ankle boots, straw bonnet, and is preserved in her original store box. $2000/3000

128. English Poured Wax Child Doll Attributed to Montanari
21" (53 cm.) Poured wax shoulder head with rounded facial shape, narrow blue glass enamel inset eyes, single stroke brows, accented nostrils, closed mouth with pouting expression, brunette inserted hair, softly stuffed muslin body, poured wax lower arms and legs, bare feet. Condition: generally excellent. Comments: attributed to Montanari, circa 1875. Value Points: especially gentle expression on the well-preserved wax doll wearing fine original multi-layered costume with fancy bonnet and silk cape with lace outline. $2000/2500

129. French Bisque Bébé Triste by Emile Jumeau with Early Costume and Signed Jumeau Shoes
22" (56 cm.) Pressed bisque socket head with very plump lower cheeks and elongated face, brown glass paperweight inset eyes, thick dark eyeliner, painted curly lashes, rose blushed eye shadow, brush-stroked and feathered brows, accented eye corners, shaded nostrils, closed mouth with defined space beween the outlined and shaded lips, separately modeled pierced ears, blonde mohair wig over cork pate, French composition and wooden eight-loose-ball jointed body with straight wrists. Condition: generally excellent. Marks: 10 (head) Jumeau Medaille d'Or Paris (body). Comments: Emile Jumeau, his signature distinctive model sculpted by noted French artist Carriere-Belleuse, circa 1884. Value Points: beautiful bébé in rarer size with wonderfully sculpted features and choice bisque, original body and body finish, beautiful early silk frock, antique undergarments, Jumeau socks, ivory satin shoes signed "Bébé Jumeau Depose 10". $14,000/18,000

130. Pair, French Silk Floral Arrangements in Original Glass Domes
16" (41 cm.) Arranged in matching porcelain vases with cobalt blue enamel coloring and gilded decorations, the matching floral displays contain a beautiful variety of blossoms and colors, and are preserved on ebony-finished

wooden bases under glass domes. French, circa 1885. Excellent condition. $300/400

131. Very Rare French Bisque Bébé E.J.A. with Original Costume and Box

25" (64 cm.) Pressed bisque socket head with elongated facial modeling, large brown glass paperweight inset eyes, thick dark eyeliner, mauve blushed eye shadow, curly dark lashes, brush-stroked and multi-feathered brows, accented eye corners, shaded nostrils, closed mouth with defined space between the shaded and outlined lips, impressed dimples at lip corners and chin, separately modeled pierced ears, blonde mohair wig over cork pate, French composition and wooden eight loose ball-jointed body with straight wrists, large lower limbs and hands, original navy blue woolen dress with cutwork trim, undergarments, silk bonnet, leather shoes signed "E. Jumeau Med d'Or Paris". Condition: generally excellent. Marks: EJ/A 10 (head) Jumeau Medaille d'Or Paris (body). Comments: Emile Jumeau, circa 1882, the rare signature model was made for two or three years only, in two sizes (10 and 11); the model was described in an early catalog as "bébé perfectionnes de Jumeau". Value Points: an outstanding example of the very rare bébé, few models exist, in impeccable original condition, original body, body finish, wig, pate, costume, shoes, and Jumeau box. $22,000/28,000

132. Fine Early Furnished Dollhouse Room with Stencilled Cabinet

13" (33 cm.) A thick wooden box-shaped room has a slanted ceiling with glass top and two back wall windows to allow natural light into the room, hinged double front doors that appear as windows when closed form a larger wing when opened. The exterior is paint-grained and stencil-outlined, with a fancy scrolled decoration at the crest. The interior has original painting with trompe d'oeil wainscot, blue painted walls, and fancily painted floor to simulate a tapestry carpet. The house is furnished with a fine selection of Biedermeier style furniture, various decorations, and two dollhouse dolls. Circa 1860, a rare style of miniature room with original finish being well preserved. $1500/2500

132 closed.

133. Trio of Three-Arm Ormolu Chandeliers

4.5" (11 cm.) suspended. 2.5" diam. Having ornate frame with rich gold leaf finish, the three-arm chandeliers have milk glass globes and fancy ceiling cap. Excellent condition. Late 19th century. $400/600

134. Pair, Very Ornate Crystal Six-Arm Chandeliers

4.5" (11 cm.) A matching pair or very ornate crystal chandeliers features dangling chains of cut crystals that suspend below the six-arm petal-shaped candle holders; dangling from each candle holder are teardrops and a large crystal ball suspends from the center. Excellent condition. 19th century. $600/900

133.

134.

135.

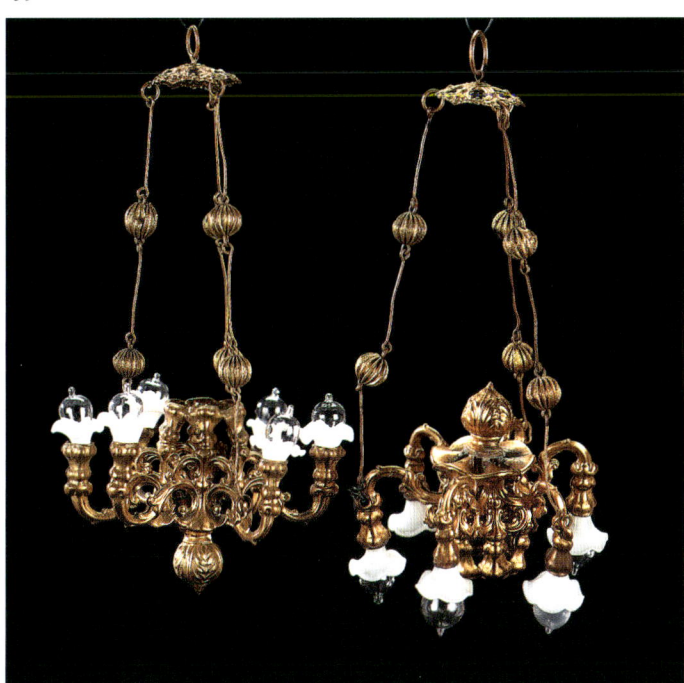

136.

135. Pair, 19th Century Cranberry Glass Chandeliers
4.5" (11 cm.) suspended. The matched pair of blown glass hanging chandeliers in graduated shades of cranberry are bell-shaped and designed to suspend by means of delicate brass chains from a matching cranberry glass ceiling cap. Excellent condition. 19th century. $800/1000

136. Pair of 19th Century Six-Arm Ormolu Chandeliers
5" (13 cm.) suspended. 3" diam. The richly gold leaf finished ormolu chandeliers with very ornate center and ceiling cap has six arms, each with milk glass tulip shaped shade. Excellent condition. Late 19th century. $400/600

137. An Outstanding Crystal Glass Doll House Chandelier
9" (23 cm.) The superb cut crystal pear-shaped chandelier with cast bronze frame has a prismatic cut glass at the center base and bronze crown with serrated top at the crest. Excellent condition. Legoland Museum of Antique Doll and Dollhouses ex-collection. Late 19th century. $900/1500

138. 19th Century Doll House Chandelier with Cut Glass Prisms
10" (25 cm.) suspended. 3"l. globe. A hemispherically shaped globe has cut glass rays with gold leaf finish and cast brass frame and candle holder. Three brackets attached to the frame have link chains that connect with a brass ceiling cap. Excellent condition. $400/600

139. Pair, Early Blown Venetian Glass Lamps
4.5" (11 cm.) The matched lamps have delicate clear glass crystal frames and are decorated with turquoise blown glass trim, with clear glass chimneys. Excellent condition. 19th century. $400/500

140. Two 19th Century Dollhouse Lamps
5" (13 cm.) Comprising two floor lamps, each with gilded ormolu base, one with circular table with garland decoration and milk glass globe with petal ruffled collar; the other with deeply embossed details and milk glass shade with brass rim. Excellent condition. Late 19th century. $400/600

141. Outstanding German Bisque Bust of Bonneted Girl with Ornately Sculpted Costume
18" (46 cm.) One piece all bisque bust of young blonde haired girl on self-pedestal, having sculpted intaglio side-glancing blue eyes, grey and black eyeliner, painted short lashes, lightly feathered brows, accented nostrils, closed mouth with outlined lips and double row of teeth, blonde sculpted hair, arms extended from torso in expressive pose. The girl has an extravagantly sculpted and decorated costume that extends all around the form, and included Dresden ruffled bonnet, gold buttons, pink and blue bows, ruffled, gilded edging, and floral decorated wide yellow bonnet bow and streamers. Excellent condition, hidden virtually imperceptible reglue of right arm behind the sleeve ruffle. Germany, circa 1890, the large size and elaborate decoration indicate its possible production as an exhibition model. $1500/2500

142. Pair, German Bisque Nodding Asian Couple
7" (18 cm.) Of fine bisque porcelain, the pair depicts a seated Asian couple with loosely attached head and hands allowing for a "nodding" action when lightly tapped. Each has elaborately sculpted costume and accessories with gilded decorations. Germany, circa 1880. Excellent condition. $500/800

143. Four German Bisque Figurines of Children
8" (20 cm.) Each is one piece figurine of child in playful standing pose, with sculpted and painted costumes, including boy and girl dancing pair, boy and girl holding a doll standing under an umbrella, and little girl carrying her younger brother. Excellent condition. Germany, Circa 1880. $300/400

144. Extremely Rare French Bisque "Statuette-Poupée" by Radiguet & Cordonnier

17" (43 cm.) Pale bisque swivel head on kid-edged bisque shoulder plate with well-defined modeled bosom and throat hollow, large grey/blue glass enamel inset eyes, dark eyeliner, painted lashes, arched feathered brows, accented nostrils, closed mouth with pale accented lips, pierced ears, very pale blonde mohair wig over cork pate, very firmly stuffed kid body with bodice cut very low to reveal modeled bisque bosom, cinched waist, kid upper arms and legs, bisque arms from above the elbows, bisque legs from above the knees with feet shaped as though wearing high heels, modeled shoes with holes in soles for positioned on original stand, antique ivory silk gown with undergarments. Condition: generally excellent. Marks: A, R,C, Depose. Comments: Radiguet & Cordonnier, circa 1880, their deposed fashion lady was named "statuette-poupée" in their 1880 registration; inspired by their theatrical costume background, the young couple sought to design a fashion lady for costume display purposes; the story of Radiguet & Cordonnier is told in detail in *The Encyclopedia of French Dolls* by Theimer. Value Points: extremely rare fashion poupée with unique sculpting of shoulder plate, arms, and bisque heeled feet, has superbly beautiful face, and her very rare original wooden base for posing. $14,000/18,000

145. Very Beautiful French Bisque Bébé Bru Jne, Size 2, by Leon Casimir Bru with Bru Shoes
13" (33 cm.) Pressed bisque swivel head on kid-edged bisque shoulder plate with modeled bosom and shoulder blades, blue glass paperweight inset eyes, dark eyeliner, curly painted lashes, arched feathered brows, accented eye corners, shaded nostrils, closed mouth with outlined lips and defined tongue tip, pierced ears, blonde mohair wig over cork pate, Bru kid bébé body with gusset-jointing at hips and knees, kid over wooden upper arms, bisque forearms and hands. Condition: generally excellent. Marks: Bru Jne 2 (head) No 2 Bru Jne (shoulders) (original Bru paper label on torso). Comments: Leon Casimir Bru, circa 1883. Value Points: especially beautiful petite Bru Jne with desirable modeled tongue tip, wonderful bisque, sturdy body, perfect hands, fine antique costume including signed Bru Jne shoes, the doll was acquired by Geri Baker from the Mildred Seeley Collection. $14,000/18,000

146. 19th Century Miniature Chest of Drawers
8" (20 cm.) Mahogany chest of drawers with rich burled wood has two large and two handkerchief drawers, each with raised edging, wooden knobs, dove-tailed construction at the front and back of drawers, and gracefully curved apron. Excellent condition. Early 19th century, fine craftsmanship. $300/500

147. French Doll's Miniature Fan with Hand-Painted Bird in Nest
3" (8 cm.) Carved bone folding fan with delicate fretwork cut-outs has interspersed blue silk panels hand-painted with colorful tiny flowers and centering a middle panel with a scene of colorfully feathered bird with nest and little eggs; the fan is edged with delicate feathers, has ormolu belt loop and is contained in original (frail) box. Excellent condition with vibrant colors. French, circa 1870. $500/800

148. French Bisque Wooden-Bodied Poupée by Maison Huret with Trunk and Trousseau
17" (43 cm.) Bisque swivel head on kid-edged bisque shoulder plate, plump facial modeling, blue glass enamel inset eyes with spiral threading, dark eyeliner, painted lashes, feathered brows, accented nostrils and eye corners, closed mouth with accented lips, pierced ears, blonde mohair wig over cork pate, all-wooden fully-articulated body with shapely torso, dowel-jointing at shoulders, elbows, wrists, hips, and knees, pivot jointing at upper legs. Condition: generally excellent. Marks: Medaille d'Argent Huret 22 Boulevard Montmartre Paris Exposition Universelle 1867 (green stamp on front torso). Comments: Maison Huret, circa 1868. Value Points: the wooden-bodied poupée has excellent posing possibilities, beautiful expression with childlike features, and is contained in an early French poupée trunk with original maker's label, along with an extensive trousseau, comprising three early gowns, capes, jacket, undergarments, bone-handled parasol, two pairs of shoes, three bonnets, and more. $15,000/20,000

149. Two French Poupée Bonnets in Signed Huret Hat Boxes
Two card paper oval boxes are stamped "Maison Hurset Boulevard Montmartre 22 Paris" on the lid and each contains a fine antique woven straw bonnet sized for 45 cm poupée, one lined with black velvet and decorated with blue silk faille ribbons, and the other lined with ivory silk satin and decorated with delicate feathers and ivory silk ribbons. Both excellent condition. French, circa 1870. $600/1000

150. Rare Danish Porcelain Lady Doll by Royal Copenhagen
13" (33 cm.) Very thick paste porcelain shoulder head with pink tinted complexion, head sculpted downward, deeply sloping shoulders, painted bright blue round eyes, black and red upper eyeliner, short feathered brows, accented nostrils, closed mouth with accent line between the rich red lips, blushed cheeks, original brunette human hair hand-tied wig, muslin torso and upper limbs, thick paste porcelain arms to above the elbows, lower legs, bare feet, cupped hands, antique gown, undergarments, bonnet, locket. Condition: generally excellent. Marks: 111 (ink script inside shoulders). Comments: Royal Copenhagen Porcelain of Denmark, circa 1850. The doll appears in *Lady Dolls of the 19th Century* by Florence Theriault. Value Points: very rare porcelain model with beautiful complexion, all original body and porcelain limbs. $3500/4500

151. Unusual 19th Century Doll's Folding Bed with Stencilled "Birds in Nest" Design
20" (51 cm.) l. 23"h. A pinewood bed has original brown painted finish, and is designed to be displayed closed, with underside of bed finished off nicely and having stenciled decoration and one working drawer with porcelain knob, or in classic bed fashion with high headboard decorated with a scene of mother bird feeding her four baby birds in a nest. The bed is neatly fitted with antique embroidered bed linens and pillow. Generally excellent, repair at foot board, small missing piece at bottom left foot. American, circa 1880. $700/900

152. English Poured Wax Doll with Original Body and Costume
17" (1 cm.) Poured wax shoulder head with blue glass eyes, painted brows and accented nostrils, closed mouth, blonde mohair tendrils of inserted hair, softly stuffed muslin body, poured wax lower arms and legs, wearing antique baby costume, undergarments, cape. Condition: generally excellent. Comments: attributed to Montanari, circa 1875. Value Points: pretty child with original body, lavish original costume. $900/1100

153. Charming French Bisque Bébé Clown, Figure A, by Jules Steiner
13" (33 cm.) Bisque socket head with untinted white clown complexion, painted red clown decorations, brown glass inset eyes, red eye outlines, curved brows, accented nostrils, closed mouth, pierced ears, blonde mohair wig, French composition five piece body, well costumed in silk and lace clown costume. Condition: generally excellent. Marks: Steiner Paris Fre A 6 (head) Le Petit Parisien (body). Comments: Jules Steiner, circa 1888. Value Points: rare model with beautiful complexion and painted clown decorations, original signed body with original finish. $2800/3800

84

154. Pair of Jumeau Shoes, Size 8

2.7" (7 cm.) Black leather shoes with brown overcast stitching at edges have brown silk bows, ankle straps with bead buttons, and soles impressed "Bébé Jumeau Depose 8". Good condition, leather scuffed. Circa 1885.
$300/400

155. Pair of Bru Shoes, Size 3

2" (5 cm.) Black soft leather shoes with brown silk ribbon banding, ankle straps, leather bows with silver buckles, tan soles impressed Bru Jne Paris and 3. Excellent condition except lacking buttons on straps. French, circa 1885.
$500/700

156. French Bisque Bébé, Size 6, by Leon Casimir Bru with Signed Shoes
18" (46 cm.) Bisque swivel head on kid-edged bisque shoulder plate, modeled bosom and shoulder blades, blue glass paperweight inset eyes, dark eyeliner, painted curly lashes, slightly modeled brush stroked brows, accented eye corners, shaded nostrils, closed mouth with outlined lips and tongue tip, pierced ears, blonde mohair wig over cork pate, kid bébé body with scalloped collarette, Chevrot hinged legs, wooden lower legs, kid over wooden upper arms, bisque forearms with sculpted bisque fingers, magenta silk dress with bustle back, silk lined cat, undergarments, stockings, leather shoes signed "Bru Jne Paris". Condition: generally excellent, two fingers reglued. Marks: Bru Jne 6 (head) Bru Jne No. 6 (shoulders). Comments: Leon Casimir Bru, circa 1886. Value Points: very pretty Bébé Bru with sought-after tongue tip model, choice bisque, sturdy original body with original Bru paper label, wonderful antique costume with signed Bru shoes.
$14,000/18,000

157. German Cloth Character in Original Tyrolean Costume by Kathe Kruse

17" (43 cm.) All cloth doll with pressed and oil painted facial features and hair, soft curls swirled onto forehead, sculpted ears, painted brown eyes with black and brown upper eyeliner, painted nostrils, closed mouth with pouting lips, stitch-jointed shoulders, disc-jointed legs, separately stitched thumbs. Condition: generally excellent except extensive paint flaking on hair at back of head. Comments: Kathe Kruse, circa 1920. Value Points: beautiful originally painted features with endearing wistful expression, wearing original grey woolen Tyrolean costume. $1700/2500

158. German Bisque Character "Hexe" in Original Costume

9" (23 cm.) Bisque socket head with sculpted wrinkles, frown lines and large red warts, black glass inset eyes, sculpted hook nose, closed mouth with sculpted crooked teeth, grey mohair wig, Sonneberg composition five piece body with painted black boots. Condition: generally excellent. Marks: Hexe 15/0. Comments: Dressel, circa 1890. Value Points: rare model with uniquely sculpted "witch" features, original costume. $1000/1500

159. German Bisque Character "Old Rip"
9" (23 cm.) Bisque socket head with incised age wrinkles and furrowed brows, black glass enamel inset eyes, long hook nose, closed mouth, high cheekbones, thickly painted brows, white mohair wig, moustache, and long flowing wig, five piece paper mache body, painted boots, original costume. Condition: generally excellent. Marks: X Old Rip 4/0. Comments: Dressel, circa 1890. Value Points: rare character story book figure with distinctively sculpted features, original wig, beard, and costume. $1000/1500

160. Earliest Period German Cloth Character by Kathe Kruse
17" (43 cm.) All cloth doll with pressed and oil painted facial features, brown sculpted hair with modeled forelock, sculpted blushed ears, small painted brown eyes with black and brown upper eyeliner, flat nose, closed mouth with downcast expression, muslin body with stitched together fingers, wearing antique cotton dress and undergarments, stockings, shoes. Condition: generally excellent. Comments: Kathe Kruse, circa 1910. Value Points: rare model with endearing poignant expression. $2200/2800

161. Very Rare Swiss Studio Doll by Sasha Morgenthaler
20" (51 cm.) Sculpted socket head with distinctive brown complexion, well-defined cheekbones, painted eyes with strongly defined eyelids, black painted eyeliner and upper lashes, single stroke brows, small nose with accented nostrils, closed mouth, black human hair, five piece body. Condition: generally excellent. Marks: Sasha (original studio wrist tag). Comments: Sasha Morgenthaler studio doll, circa 1950s. Value Points: extremely rare studio model wearing her original beautifully detailed soft kidskin costume with fur, braid, and embroidered trim. $3500/6500

162. Very Rare American Paper Mache Black Character Child Attributed to Leo Moss
17" (43 cm.) Hand-pressed paper mache head with flanged neck, rich black complexion and hair, sculpted very tight short curly hair with details of curls tumbling onto the forehead, sculpted angled black brows, heavily lidded inset brown eyes with black eyeliner, broad rounded nose, closed mouth with full pouting downcast lips, very plump cheeks, three modelled tears on cheeks as though falling from eyes, brown muslin torso and upper legs, composition lower limbs, wearing white cotton dress, undergarments, shoes, stockings. Condition: generally excellent. Marks: 1901 LM. Comments: attributed to Leo Moss, circa 1901, the itinerant black carpenter of Georgia is believed to have created a small number of one-of-a-kind dolls depicting children of his small town world; his materials were those found-at-hand, for example the left-over scraps of wall paper from his day job. The tearful faced children were signature to his style, and each was created uniquely. Value Points: rare American doll with outstanding sculpting and portraiture, enhanced by the mysterious background of the artist, superb state of preservation. $4000/6000

163. German Miniature Woven Doll Carriage with All Porcelain Doll
8" (20 cm.) Woven wicker baby carriage with fancy sides has four spoked soft metal wheels, wire curved handle and wooden hand grip, leather hinged sunshade with matching leather blanket cover. Along with all porcelain character doll with painted black baby hair and well-defined features, in antique costume. Condition: generally excellent. Comments: Germany, circa 1880. Value Points: rarer model of miniature doll carriage with all intact original fittings, sweet-faced doll. $700/1000

164. American Paper Mache Sleeping Baby "Danny" Attributed to Leo Moss

15" (38 cm.) Paper mache head with flanged neck depicting a sleeping black-complexioned baby, having sculpted short hair with very tight curls, sculpted closed eyes with painted lower lashes, modeled thick brows with black painted details, broad rounded nose, very full lips of closed mouth, midnight brown muslin body, composition lower limbs, antique baby dress and antique patchwork quilt. Condition: generally excellent. Marks: LM (head) Danny 1919 (handwritten tag stitched to chest). Comments: attributed to Leo Moss, the itinerant handyman who is believed to have created the series of black children representing youngsters from his Georgia home town, some representing his own children, at the beginning of the 20th century. Value Points: artful and endearing portrait of sleeping child is beautifully preserved. $2000/3000

165. Two German Metal Painted Miniature Beds by Maerklin

6" (15 cm.) Each is metal bed with curved head and foot board and elaborate scrolled inserts, with metal coin springs, and fitted with mattress and quilt, one with original blue paint and gilt stencil, the other with cream paint and gilt stencil. Excellent condition. Germany, Maerklin, circa 1900. $400/500

166. Grand English Wooden Lady Doll with Enamel Eyes
27" (69 cm.) Carved wooden head and torso, egg-shaped head, elongated strong throat, modeled bosom and tiny waist, flat back torso, black enamel inset eyes with dot-painted lashes and brows, distinctively carved nose, blush spots on cheeks, painted mouth with center accent line, wooden lower arms with separately carved fingers, cloth upper arms, wooden dowel-jointed legs, wearing early silk gown with attached stomacher, hemp wig, and carrying early carved bone fan with silk blades. Condition: generally very good, some restoration to forehead and left side of face (under wig), and gesso worn at back of head under the wig. Comments: English, late 18th century, the doll was previously owned by Ruth and Robert Mathes, and appeared in their book, Dolls, Toys and Childhood, page 56, before being acquired by Geri Baker. Value Points: grand size of the early wooden lady with well-defined features artfully clustered at the center face. $8000/12,000

167. Early English Painting "Little Girls with Doll at a Tea Party"
14" (36 cm.) x 10". Painting on canvas depicts two young girls in a garden setting, one seated at a miniature table pouring tea in a child-sized tea set, the other holding her doll. The painting details are exquisite including coral necklace on one girl, dog seated at their side, the corner of a porch at one side, playing cards strewn across the table and tumbling to the ground, very pleasing faces on girls, and a fine early classic English wooden doll with flat back, modeled bosom, period costume. The delicate watercolor is varnished (originally) and is presented in its early frame under glass. Excellent condition, unsigned, circa 1810. $2500/3500

168. Set Miniature Leather Bound Volumes of Shakespeare
3" (8 cm.) x 2". Ten soft bound leather volumes with gold tooled lettering on the covers, are various plays of Williams Shakespeare, "carefully edited and compared with the best texts", each with an engraving of the author on the first page. Published by Knickerbocker Leather and Novelty Co, New York. Good condition, some loose spines, leather fading. Early 20th century. $300/500

169. Early 19th Century Lady's Toilette Table
15" (38 cm.) l. 10"h. The gracefully shaped furniture, appearing as a desk when closed, has rich marquetry inlays of fine woods, cabriole legs, shaped apron front, and dove-tailed wooden drawer. The top is separated into three sections, viz. a central panel that folds up to reveal a mirror and table surface, and two side arms that fold outward to reveal deep compartments. Excellent condition. The use of fine woods and expert craftsmanship indicate a maitrise model. Early 19th century. $1200/1800

170. English Poured Wax Child Doll in Original Costume and Box
20" (51 cm.) Poured wax shoulder head with lovely pink tinted complexion, blue glass inset eyes, painted lashes and brows, closed mouth with accented lips, delicate tendrils of inserted hair, softly stuffed muslin body, poured wax lower limbs, bare feet. Condition: generally excellent. Comments: attributed to Montanari, circa 1870. Value Points: wearing original very elaborate lace gown and bonnet, the doll is presented in her original wooden box with ink-script note torn from an old letter and pasted on the inside lid "Brought from London, England to Ellen Maria (blank) by her father in 1854". $1200/1800

171. Very Early and Fine Miniature English Slant-Front Desk with Maker's Mark
7.5" (19 cm.) h. x 6"w. x 3"d. The dark walnut desk has three drawers with red paper lining, tiny metal ball knobs, the upper drawer slightly narrower and shorter allowing space for the pull-out supports for desk surface when opened, slant top that hinges open to reveal a neatly fitted interior with two pull-out drawers and fancy cornice. The hand-cast brass-plated hardware includes four faux-locks. The name "J. Bubbs Maker" is impressed on the base. Excellent condition, left leg apron missing. English, late 18th century, a very rare early miniature furnishing with maker's signature. $1200/1800

172. Early Wooden Doll's Bed with Iron Canopy
24" (61 cm.) h. 18"l. A wooden doll-sized bed with wooden springs, steeple shaped head and foot boards and tapered legs is fitted with early white pique coverlet, and surmounted by an original gracefully curved cast iron canopy frame with circular wooden cap. Excellent condition. Early 19th century. $1100/1700

173. 18th Century English Wooden Doll with Fine Period Costume
20" (51 cm.) Carved wooden one piece head and torso with egg-shaped head, elongated throat, defined bosom, flat torso back, carved nose, tiny carved definition of chin, blue enamel inset eyes, tiny dot painted lashes, widely arched dot painted brows, closed mouth with center accent line, curly grey hair on original tacked on linen cap, wooden legs with jointing at hips and knees, cloth upper arms, hand-stitched kid hands, wearing fine early homespun gown with

transfer painted designs, undergarments, ruffled bonnet. Condition: generally good, original and unrestored, large paint flake on cheek and at back neck. Comments: England, circa 1780. Value Points: beautifully painted features include delicate eye decoration and subtle blushing of cheeks, fine costume. $8000/12,000

174. Early Walnut Spinning Wheel with Bone Finials
11" (28 cm.) A walnut treadle spinning wheel with working parts is beautifully crafted with alternating ebony finished spindles and trim, and having three bone tear-shaped finials. Excellent condition. Mid-19th century. $600/900

175. Large Wooden Georgian Style House with Balustrade and Wedgewood Room
50" (127 cm.) h. x 44"w. x 20"d. The large two story wooden house has 10 glass windows with defined wood panel panes, and 2 arched French doors at the sides that open onto attached railed balconies. A balustrade with fancily carved spindles runs around the flat room top. The four interior rooms have varnished wooden floors, and there is a fireplace in each 1st floor room. The living room is painted wedgewood blue and is decorated with 14 oval or round porcelain Wedgewood cameos with various designs. Very good condition. English, circa 1840. $5000/7500

176. German Bisque Doll House Man with Ornately Sculpted Helmet
8" (20 cm.) Bisque shoulder head with black sculpted hair beneath a very high black helmet or cap decorated lavishly with red braid and tassels, painted facial features, brown moustache, muslin body, bisque lower limbs, painted boots, wearing original regimental costume. Condition: generally excellent. Comments: Germany, circa 1890. Value Points: rare doll house figure with exceptional detail of sculpted helmet. $600/900

177. Three German All-Bisque Soldiers with Modeled Helmets
3" (8 cm.) Each has one piece bisque head and torso, sculpted military helmet, painted facial features and hair, sculpted moustache, jointed arms and legs, black boots. Condition: generally excellent. Comments: Germany, circa 1890, from a series, each has variation of helmet style and painting, and wears its factory original felt regimental costume with elaborate braid. $600/900

178. Set, German Dollhouse Furnishings with Original Paper Decorations
5" (13 cm.) h. cupboard. Each of the matched ensemble is of light pinewood with lithographed paper cover to simulate fancy stenciled painting, the chairs and settee with original blue velvet cover and gilt paper edging. The set comprises settee, four side chairs, round pedestal table, cupboard with window-door top, cupboard with shelved top, and hall mirror with cupboard base. Excellent condition, brilliant colors of paper design. Germany, circa 1890. $800/1200

179. German All-Bisque Dollhouse Man and Horse
5" (13 cm.) Bisque shoulder head with black sculpted hair and moustache, painted facial features, muslin body, bisque lower limbs, painted boots, wearing brown woolen great coat with cap, and trousers. Along with his carved wooden hide-covered horse with tiny black bead eyes, mane, tail, and elaborate saddle, stirrups, harness and blanket pad. Condition: generally excellent. Comments: Germany, circa 1890. Value Points: rare moustache man, wonderful detail of miniature horse and accessories. $400/600

180. Very Ornate Tudor Style Doll House
38" (97 cm.) h. x 36"w. x 23"d. A light-wood dollhouse has faux-brick finish and applied wood trim at all corners to simulate stone. There is a wrap-around porch with four

carved columns and a fancily spindled railing; and a second floor balcony, seven exterior steps lead to the extremely ornate front door with decorative fan light, and there is lattice at the roof peak and edges, 2 chimneys and 21 windows including 3 "stained glass" windows. The interior two stories have four rooms with central staircase, lithographed tile floors throughout, and floral wall paper. Fair condition, a beautiful house in as found condition, worthy of restoration. Late 19th century. $2000/2500

181. Four German Bisque Doll House Dolls with Sculpted Hair
6" (15 cm.) largest. Each has bisque or china shoulder head with sculpted hair and painted facial features, muslin body, bisque lower limbs, painted shoes. Condition: generally excellent, one with chipped foot. Comments: Germany, circa 1880. Value Points: well sculpted hair, with original bodies and original costumes including three boys. $400/600

◆ 95 ◆

182. Fabulous Collection of 54 Czech Puppets
7" (18 cm.) 54 paper mache puppets, each with uniquely sculpted head, and hair, painted facial features and hair with head-dress or cap, has loosely-jointed wooden and paper mache body with painted shoes and original fabric costume, and each is attached to metal rod with wooden handle and strings. Condition: generally excellent. Marks: AMP (with clown logo) Munzbergo Vy Loutky (paper label on handles of some). Comments: Czech, the tradition of puppet theatre in that Eastern Europe country is centuries old, and during the early 20th century it literally burgeoned, with the creation of hundreds of small theatre groups throughout the villages, and even an International Puppetry Exhibition in 1929. Value Points: the extensive collection, each character varies, is perfectly preserved, and includes an additional 23 heads and various parts. $3500/5500

183. Superb and Rare French Bisque Bébé Jumeau, Incised Depose, in Grand Size 20 with Antique Costume
40" (102 cm.) Bisque socket head, blue glass paperweight inset eyes, dark eyeliner, lushly painted lashes, rose blushed eye shadow, widely arched brush-stroked brows, accented eye corners, shaded nostrils, closed mouth, outlined lips, pierced ears, blonde human hair wig, French composition and wooden fully-jointed body. Condition: generally excellent, some body retouch. Marks: Depose Jumeau 20 (incised mark, and artist checkmarks). Comments: Emile Jumeau, circa 1885, the incised depose model was made for one year only and very few examples in this largest size, 20, are known to exist. Value Points: very rare doll is enhanced by beautiful bisque and painting, original Jumeau body, antique white pique boy's suit. $15,000/22,000

184. French Bisque Block Letter Bébé by Gaultier in Size 16 with Original Body
42" (107 cm.) Bisque socket head with plump facial modeling, large blue glass paperweight inset eyes, dark eyeliner, painted lashes, rose blushed eye shadow, brush-stroked and multi-feathered brows, closed mouth with tiny modeled tongue tip, accent line between the lips, pierced ears, brunette human hair wig over cork pate, French composition and wooden fully jointed body with straight wrists. Condition: generally excellent. Marks: F. 16 G. Comments: Gaultier, circa 1884. Value Points: rarer early block letter bébé in exceptional size, has lovely expression and bisque, original body and body finish, wearing superb antique white pique dress, undergarments, straw bonnet. $7000/10,000

185. 19th Century Large Pull Toy Lamb on Wooden Platform
26" (66 cm.) Paper mache lamb with very lush lambswool fleecy coat has canvas face with painted eyes and mouth, canvas covered wooden legs, and is mounted upon a red wooden wheeled platform. Excellent condition. Late 19th century. $900/1300

186. German Bisque Toddler, 247, by Kestner in Large Size
28" (71 cm.) Bisque socket head, brown glass sleep eyes, thick eyeliner, painted curly lashes, short feathered brows, accented nostrils, open mouth, outlined lips, two porcelain upper teeth, brunette human hair bobbed wig, composition and wooden ball-jointed toddler body with side-hip jointing, wearing antique white pique jacket with cutwork collar, trousers, knit stockings, leather shoes. Condition: generally excellent. Marks: P made in Germany 19 JDK 247 19. Comments: Kestner, circa 1914. Value Points: fine large size of the cheerful toddler known as "Baby Jean" with fine luminous bisque, impressed dimples. $1100/1800

187. German Bisque Toddler, 247, by Kestner with Original Paper Label
20" (51 cm.) Bisque socket head, blue glass sleep eyes, painted curly lashes, incised eyeliner, short feathered brows, accented nostrils and eye corners, open mouth, two porcelain upper teeth, tongue, brunette human hair bobbed wig over original plaster pate, composition and wooden ball-jointed toddler body with side hip-jointing, nicely costumed. Condition: generally excellent. Marks: K made in Germany 14 247 JDK 14. Comments: Kestner, circa 1914. Value Points: wonderful sculpting with deeply impressed cheek dimples, fine quality of bisque, toddler body, with original Kestner paper label. $1200/1700

188. German Bisque Character, 604, by Bahr and Proschild
11" (28 cm.) Bisque socket head, brown glass sleep eyes, painted curly lashes, short feathered brows, accented nostrils and eye corners, closed mouth with two beaded upper teeth, brunette mohair bobbed wig, composition bent limb baby body. Condition: generally excellent. Marks: B.P. (crossed swords) 604 2. Comments: Bahr and Proschild, circa 1915. Value Points: pretty character toddler well defined features, original body finish. Well-detailed antique costume. $600/900

189. Rare German Bisque Character, 141, by Hertel and Schwab

19" (48 cm.) Bisque socket head, blue glass sleep eyes, painted curly lashes, short feathered brows, accented nostrils and eye corners, open mouth, outlined lips, four porcelain teeth, brunette hand-tied human hair wig, composition and wooden ball-jointed body. Condition: generally excellent. marks: 141 6. Comments: Hertel and Schwab, circa 1912. Value Points: rare model with wonderfully expressive features, antique costume, fine bisque. $3000/4000

190. Fine German Bisque Character, 117x, by Kammer and Reinhardt

14" (36 cm.) Bisque socket head, blue glass sleep and flirty eyes, mohair lashes, dark eyeliner, painted lashes, short feathered brows, open mouth, four tiny porcelain teeth, auburn mohair wig, composition and wooden ball-jointed flapper body with side-hip jointing and above the knee jointed lower legs, antique costume. Condition: generally excellent. Marks: K*R Simon & Halbig 117x Germany 34. Comments: Kammer and Reinhardt, circa 1915. Value Points: rare variation of the 117 model with unusual expression, fine bisque, original body and body finish. $800/1200

191. German Bisque Character, 249, by Kestner

15" (38 cm.) Bisque socket head, brown glass sleep eyes, mohair lashes, painted curly lashes, short feathered brows, accented nostrils and eye corners, open mouth, shaded and outlined lips, four porcelain teeth, brunette mohair wig, composition and wooden ball-jointed body, antique costume. Condition: generally excellent. Marks: B made in Germany 6 JDK 249 6. Comments: Kestner, circa 1915, the model known as "Hilda's older sister". Value Points: rarely found model appears as an older version of the tradename Hilda doll, has lovely matte bisque and painting. $800/1200

192. French Bisque Bébé Jumeau, Size 11, with Original Chemise and Shoes

24" (61 cm.) Bisque socket head, blue glass paperweight inset eyes, dark eyeliner, painted lashes, rose blushed eye shadow, brush-stroked and multi-feathered brows, accented eye corners and nostrils, closed mouth with outlined lips, pierced ears, blonde mohair wig over cork pate, French composition and wooden fully-jointed body. Condition: generally excellent. Marks: Depose Tete Jumeau Bte SGDG 11 (head) Jumeau Medaille d'Or Paris (body). Comments: Emile Jumeau, circa 1888. Value Points: pretty bébé with creamy bisque, very deep paperweight eyes, original body, body finish, wig, Jumeau flowered chemise, blue knit stockings, leather shoes with Paris Depose 11 with bee symbol. $4500/5500

193. French Bisque Bébé Jumeau, Size 1

9" (23 cm.) Bisque socket head, blue glass paperweight inset eyes, lushly painted lashes, brushstroked and multi-feathered brows, accented nostrils and eye corners, closed mouth with outlined lips, pierced ears, blonde mohair wig over cork pate, French composition and wooden fully-jointed body. Condition: 3/4" old hairline at mid-forehead from rim, large earlobe chip, one hand repainted. Marks: Depose Tete Jumeau Bte SGDG 1 (and artist's checkmarks, on head). Comments: Emile Jumeau, circa 1888. Value Points: wonderful little size 1 bébé has original (frail) wig, Jumeau earrings, signed Jumeau body. $2000/2500

194. French Bisque Poupée by Gaultier in Original Folklore Costume
15" (38 cm.) Bisque swivel head on kid-edged bisque shoulder plate, blue glass enamel inset eyes, painted lashes and brows, accented nostrils and eye corners, closed mouth with accented lips, pierced ears, brunette human hair over cork pate, original French muslin poupée body with kid arms, separately stitched fingers. Condition: generally excellent, very tiny pinflake in right eye corner, finger tips worn on left hand. Comments: Gaultier, circa 1885. Value Points: lovely poupée with very sturdy original body, wears her beautifully preserved original folklore costume with silk striped apron and matching coiffe, velvet jacket and skirt edging, "emerald" earrings and cross, leather slippers. $2500/3500

195. Petite French Bisque Bébé Jumeau, Size 2, in Original Chemise
11" (28 cm.) Bisque socket head, blue glass paperweight inset eyes, lushly painted dark lashes, brush-stroked and multi-feathered brows, accented eye corners, shaded nostrils, closed mouth with shaded and outlined lips, pierced ears, blonde mohair wig over cork pate, French composition and wooden fully-jointed body. Condition: generally excellent. Marks: Depose Tete Jumeau Bte SGDG 2 (head) Jumeau Medaille d'Or Paris (body). Comments: Emile Jumeau, circa 1886. Value Points: beautiful painting on the petite bébé, with original wig, pate, body, body finish, and wearing original earrings and chemise. $3500/4500

196. French Bisque Bébé Jumeau, in Original Costume with Decorative Box
25" (64 cm.) Bisque socket head, blue glass paperweight inset eyes, dark eyeliner, lushly painted brows, accented eye corners, shaded nostrils, closed mouth with outlined lips, pierced ears, blonde mohair wig over cork pate, French composition and wooden fully-jointed body. Condition: generally excellent. Marks: Depose Tete Jumeau Bte SGDG 11 (and artist checkmarks, head) Jumeau Medaille d'Or Paris (body). Comments: Emile Jumeau, circa 1890. Value Points: having fine creamy bisque enhancing the plumply modeled cheeks, original wig, body, body finish, and wearing lovely original department store costume and leather shoes, along with richly decorated colorful silk-lined wooden box in which the bébé was first presented to a young Spanish girl in 1894. $4500/5500

198. German Bisque Toddler, "Phillip", 115/A, by Kammer and Reinhardt

15" (38 cm.) Bisque socket head, blue glass sleep eyes, painted curly lashes, short feathered brows, accented nostrils of upturned nose, closed mouth with downcast pouting lips, brunette mohair bobbed wig, composition and wooden ball-jointed toddler body with side-hip jointing, antique romper suit, leather shoes, socks. Condition: generally excellent. Marks: K*R Simon & Halbig 115/A 38. Comments: Kammer and Reinhardt, their character model marketed as "Phillip", circa 1912. Value Points: especially fine quality of modeling and fine matte bisque, original wig, body. $3000/3500

199. German Bisque Toddler, 122, by Kammer and Reinhardt

20" (51 cm.) Bisque socket head, blue glass sleep eyes, dark eyeliner, painted curly lashes, brush-stroked and feathered brows, accented nostrils and eye corners, open mouth, outlined lips, two porcelain upper teeth, tongue, brunette human hair in bobbed fashion, composition and wooden ball-jointed toddler body with side-hip jointing. Condition: generally excellent. Marks: K*R Simon & Halbig 122 42. Comments: Kammer and Reinhardt, circa 1915. Value Points: unusually expressive features enhanced by fine luminous complexion, original toddler body with original finish, antique costume. $400/600

200. German Bisque Toddler, 121, by Kammer and Reinhardt

17" (43 cm.) Bisque socket head, brown glass sleep eyes, dark eyeliner, painted lashes, short brush-stroked brows with feathered details, accented nostrils, open mouth, shaded and outlined lips, two porcelain upper teeth, tongue, blonde flocked hair, composition and wooden ball-jointed toddler body with side-hip jointing, velvet Sunday Best ensemble with matching cap, leather ankle boots. Condition: generally excellent. marks: K*R Simon & Halbig 121. Comments: Kammer and Reinhardt, circa 1920. Value Points: appealing character with toddler body. $400/500

197. German Bisque Flapper Lady with High-Heeled Feet, 1159, by Simon and Halbig

13" (33 cm.) Bisque socket head, blue glass sleep eyes, painted lashes, feathered brows, accented nostrils and eye corners, open mouth, four teeth, pierced ears, brunette mohair bobbed wig, composition and wooden slender body with flapper styling, elongated limbs with ball-jointing at shoulders, hips and above the knees, flapper style costume. Condition: generally excellent. Marks: 1159 Simon & Halbig S&H 5. Comments: Simon and Halbig, circa 1915. Value Points: sought-after model with unique original body, original wig. $900/1300

201. Extremely Rare German Bisque Lady, Size 19, by Simon and Halbig
46" (117 cm.) Bisque socket head with unusual elongated oval shape, blue glass sleep eyes, human hair lashes, dark eye liner, painted dark curly lashes, modeled detail of brows with brush-stroked painting, accented eye corners, shaded nostrils, open mouth, shaded and outlined lips, four porcelain teeth, pierced ears, long brunette wig, composition and wooden ball-jointed body, wearing lovely antique mauve silk taffeta lady's gown, undergarments, bonnet, shoes. Condition: generally excellent, body finish original with some revarnish. Marks: 1079 S&H dep 19 (head) Wimpern (stamp). Comments: Simon & Halbig, circa 1900. Value Points: extremely rare largest size of Simon and Halbig doll, with unusual facial shape, lovely bisque and painting. $3500/4500

202. Very Rare German Bisque Characters, "Max" and "Moritz" by Kammer and Reinhardt

16" (41 cm.) Each has bisque socket head with unique and highly characterized facial features depicting a mischievous urchin, brown or blue glass sleep and flirty eyes, painted fringed upper lashes, modeled comma-shaped arched brows, rounded nose, closed mouth with devilish smile, accented lips, dimpled cheeks and philtrum, mohair wig, composition fully-jointed body with sculpted and painted shoes and socks. Condition: generally excellent. Marks: K*R Simon & Halbig 123 (or 124). Comments: Kammer and Reinhardt, circa 1915, depicted are the characters "Max" and "Moritz" from the original children's stories by German Wilhelm Busch; although written in the mid-19th century the stories remained popular favorites until well into the 20th century and were the inspiration for the American comic strip characters in The Katzenjammer Kids. Research indicates the doll models may have been created and marketed to promote that series. Value Points: outstanding quality of modeling, bisque and painting on the very rare characters, each with distinctive characteristics from the other, and used for no other model, with distinctive bodies created for these dolls only. Few pairs of the rare dolls are known to exist. $40,000/55,000

203. Pair, Swiss Metal and Paper Mache Comic Character Dolls by Bucherer

6.5" (17 cm.) and 8". Each has paper mache head depicting a highly characterized person with wide googly eyes, arched brows, over-sized nose, wide sculpted moustache, one lean with black hair and sculpted cap, the other short and pudgy with bald pate; each with all-metal body constructed in an intricate manner with ball-bearings allowing infinite articulation, paper mache hands with posed fingers in different manner. Condition: generally excellent. Marks: Bucherer Made in Switzerland. Comments: Bucherer, the Swiss clock and watch maker created a series of comical dolls, circa 1920, with unique metal ball-bearing bodies; this pair depict the comic strip characters Mutt and Jeff. Value Points: wonderful original condition of the caricature pair, each with original felt costume, and celluloid button; Jeff's pin saying "I'm the guy that done it all", and Mutt's pin "On your way". $700/1100

204. Pair, American Wooden Comic Characters by Schoenhut

8" (20 cm.) Each is all wooden, depicting the comic strip characters, Barney Google and Spark Plug, with painted features and jointed limbs; Barney Google with very large O-shaped googly eyes and long pointed nose, painted moustache, wooden top hat and wearing black and white checkered pants, black felt jacket, shirt and red bow tie; Spark Plug with black O-shaped eyes, painted harness, wearing mustard-yellow felt horse black lettered Spark Plug. Condition: generally excellent. Marks: Copyright 1922 King Features Syndicate Pat Applied For. Comments: Schoenhut, circa 1922, depicted are the popular early comic strip characters, Barney Google and Spark Plug. $700/900

205. Compelling and Rare German Art Character Doll by Marian Kaulitz

18" (46 cm.) Hand-sculpted composition socket head, painted dark blue eyes in deep eye sockets, modeled eyelids with outline, lightly feathered brows, accented nostrils and eye corners, closed mouth with defined space between the accented lips, defined chin and cheek bones, well-sculpted ears, brunette mohair wig, composition and wooden ball-jointed body, antique costume, undergarments, shoes. Condition: generally excellent. Comments: Marian Kaulitz introduced her new concept "art character reform" dolls in 1908 to counteract the dolls then being marketed which she considered too pretty and unrealistic; her concept is believed to be the inspiration for the character doll movement that swept the industry for the ensuing decade. Value Points: an especially appealing character model with beautiful original complexion and painting, wonderful characterization, original body and body finish. $3500/4500

206. German Cloth Character "Edouard" by Steiff with Original Costume
20" (51 cm.) All wool felt doll with swivel head, center seam face, blue enamel eyes, mask pressed features with rounded upturned nose, stitched lips and ears, fleeced blonde/grey hair, slender body with jointed arms and legs, large cobbled leather boots. Condition: good, surface dust, some moth holes in costume. Marks: Steiff (button in ear). Comments: Steiff, circa 1913, "Edouard" the "tennis man", circa 1913, was introduced as the partner of "Bette". Value Points: rare early Steiff model with highly characterized features, wonderfully cobbled leather shoes. $1200/1800

207. German Cloth Character "Bette" by Steiff
18" (46 cm.) All felt doll with swivel head, center-seamed face, black bead eyes, mask-shaped face with tinted facial features, brunette mohair wig, tall slender body, jointed arms and legs, sewn on brown felt gloves, leather shoes, wearing original white wool felt tennis ensemble. Condition: fair, elements of costume are missing including hat. Marks: Steiff (button in ear). Comments: Steiff, circa 1913, "Bette", the "tennis lady", first model introduced with "combable" hair, tennis racquets were available separately. Value Points: rare early Steiff model with firm body, is well-preserved, has original well-cobbled shoes. $1200/1800

208. Small German Cloth Character Doll by Steiff
10" (25 cm.) All felt doll with swivel head, center seam face, blue glass eyes, pressed features, stitched mouth and ears, grey mohair wig, jointed shoulders and hips, wearing original blue felt trousers and cap, striped cotton shirt, wooden shoes. Condition: very good. Marks: Steiff (button in ear). Comments: Steiff, circa 1912. Value Points: well-preserved condition of the little tyke with endearing expression. $900/1300

209. Swiss Wooden Character Doll in Original Folklore Costume
11" (28 cm.) Carved wooden socket head with carved details of hair having braided ringlets at the sides of face, painted blue upper glancing eyes, black upper eyeliner and brows, accented nostrils, closed mouth with accented lips, all-wooden body jointed at shoulders and hips. Condition: generally excellent. Comments: Switzerland, circa 1925. Value Points: the little doll wears her original folklore costume including black velvet cap. $500/800

210. German Cloth Character Doll "Bellhop" by Steiff

20" (51 cm.) All felt wool doll with swivel head, center seam face, blue bead eyes, long pointy nose, uptilted head, stitched mouth and ears, auburn fleecy wig, elongated body with jointed shoulders and hips, oversized feet with leather boots. Condition: very good, some typical dust, fading. Marks: Steiff (button in ear). Comments: Steiff, circa 1913, "thin" style Bellhop with red woolen jacket with trim, matching brimmed cap, grey fitted trousers. Value Points: rare early cloth doll with amusingly characterized features. $2000/3000

211. Early Paper Mache Peddler Lady Doll with Dolls and Novelties

20" (51 cm.) Paper mache shoulder head depicting an aged lady with impressed wrinkles, blue glass inset eyes, strong nose and chin, slightly parted lips with spaced teeth, brunette human hair wig, linen body, posable arms, wearing original red woolen gown with black velvet trim, matching hooded cape, undergarments, hand-cobbed leather boots. Condition: generally excellent. Comments: circa 1850. Value Points: the kindly smiling peddler lady wears spectacles, has original costume and carries a well-laden tray with a wide variety of dolls, toys and decorative novelties, viz. more than eight different dolls, harmonica, locket, books, silhouette in frame, fine necessaire with gold-plated scissors, and more. $1100/1500

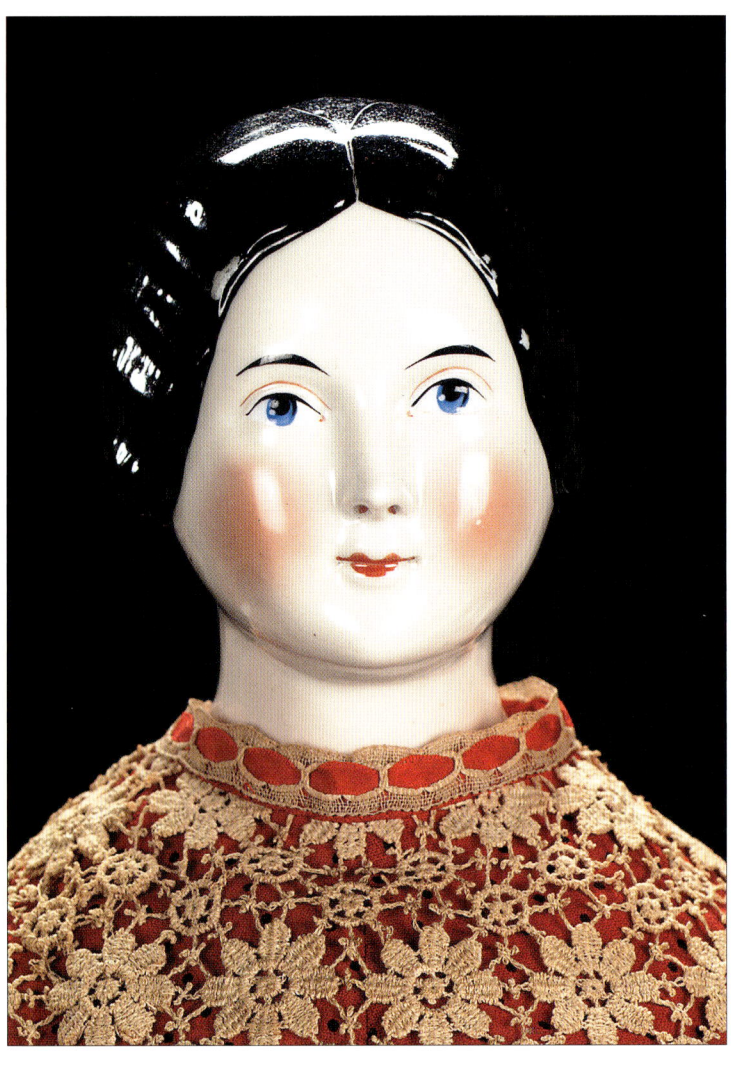

212. Early German Porcelain Lady with Refined Presence

26" (66 cm.) overall. 7"l. head. Pink tinted thick porcelain shoulder head with full oval face, strong elongated throat, black sculpted hair with center-part drawn smoothly around the sides of face and into a six-strand coiled braid at the back, large painted blue eyes in defined eye sockets, thick black upper eyeliner, red eyeliner, single stroke brows, aquiline nose with circle accents, closed mouth with very tentative smile, muslin stitch-jointed body with elongated legs, porcelain hands, antique woolen dress with cotton lace, undergarments, leather shoes. Condition: generally excellent, hands restored, two original firing lines at back sew holes. Comments: Germany, circa 1860. Value Points: early model in fine larger size with beautiful features and lustrous pink-tinted complexion. $900/1300

213. German Porcelain Doll with Original Costume

Porcelain shoulder head with rounded facial shape and solid dome, sloping shoulders, painted blue eyes, red and black upper eyeliner, single stroke brows, circle accents at nostrils, closed mouth with pert smile, brunette human hair wig, muslin stitch-jointed body, porcelain limbs, antique costume. Condition: generally excellent. Comments: Germany, circa 1880. Value Points: pretty child doll with pleasing patina of complexion. $800/1000

214. Three Miniature German Porcelain Dolls with Wooden Articulated Bodies

4.5" (11 cm.) Each has porcelain shoulder head with black sculpted hair, two with short finger curls and one with short boyish hair ending in stippled curls at the forehead, painted facial features, wooden body with shapely torso, dowel-jointing at shoulders, elbows, hips and knees, the two girls with porcelain lower arms and legs, painted flat shoes. Contained in antique cardboard valise. Condition: generally excellent, boy's lower limbs

may not be original. Comments: Germany, circa 1850. Value Points: rare models in appealing dollhouse size. $900/1300

215. Miniature Wooden Doll's Secretarie with Porcelain Figurines
9" (23 cm.) h. 2" figurines. A wooden upright desk in the Empire manner has a drop front to reveal six small maple wood drawers centering a mirrored niche, an upper drawer, and three lower drawers. Included with the desk are two fine bisque miniature figures depicting a little boy and girl training their puppies to perform tricks. Excellent condition. Mid-19th century. $700/1000

216. German Porcelain Doll with Wooden Articulated Body
9.5" (24 cm.) Pink-tinted porcelain shoulder head with slender oval face, elongated throat, black sculpted hair drawn smoothly around the face into coiled chignon, painted facial features, blue eyes, one stroke brows, accented nostrils, closed mouth, all-wooden fully articulated body with dowel-jointing, porcelain lower limbs with painted pink stocking ribbons and black flat shoes, early purple silk dress and bonnet included. Condition: generally excellent, some overpaint to fingers on right hand. Comments: Germany, circa 1859. Value Points: lovely size of the early porcelain lady with rare articulated wooden body. $2000/3000

217. German Porcelain Doll Known as "Grape Lady"
21" (53 cm.) Porcelain shoulder head of adult lady with slender oval face and elongated throat, black sculpted hair captured beneath a sculpted snood with gilt decorated white frame and a cluster of grapes at the crown, painted blue eyes, red and black upper eyeliner, single strong brows, accented nostrils and eye corners, closed mouth with center accent line, muslin stitch-jointed body with (new) porcelain limbs, lovely antique gown and undergarments. Condition: generally excellent. Comments: Germany, circa 1870. Value Points: rare coiffure with fancily sculpted coiffe, demure yet elegant pose. $900/1400

218. Superb Burled Rosewood and Enamel Miniature Chest
4" (10 cm.) A square shaped miniature chest of finest exotic woods has center-opening front doors to reveal a three-drawer interior; the chest is elaborately decorated with intricate and tiny enameled figures and designs on all four sides, inside and outside of doors, and drawer fronts, has four intricate feet, and spiral rope pillars at each corners. 19th century, superb quality of workmanship. Excellent condition. $700/1000

219. Pair of Miniature French Art Glass Vases, One Signed Daum Nancy
1.5" (4 cm.) - 2 1/2". Comprising two acid-etched art glass vases, one in shades of mauve with leafless tree and forest in the background, signed Daum Nancy; the other in shades of blue depicting a village scene at the seaside, signed in gold. French, circa 1920. Excellent condition. $500/800

220. Three Silver Miniature Chairs with "Surprise" Seats
5.5" (14 cm.) Two high-back chairs and a matching settee are of elaborate fretwork silver plated metal, and have unusual "sunken" seats covered with velvet upholstery; the seats lift off to reveal the hidden recess compartment below. Excellent condition. 19th century. $400/500

221. German Miniature Porcelain Bust by K.P.M.
4" (10 cm.) Fine white porcelain bust depicting refined lady with brown flowing hair and very

110

elaborate costume and coiffure is presented on a white porcelain plinth with gold stencilling. Marked K.P.M. Excellent condition. 19th century. $400/500

222. Collection of Miniature Porcelain-Painted Enamels

1.7" (4 cm.) Comprising a series of four oval enamels with hand-painted battle scenes in exquisite miniature detail, along with miniature painted enamel portraits (with button hook back) possibly depicting Napoleon and Josephine. Early 19th century. Excellent condition. $800/1000

223. Splendid French Bisque Bébé A.T. by Andre Thuillier with Bisque Hands

16" (41 cm.) Pressed bisque swivel head on kid-edged bisque shoulder plate, blue glass paperweight inset eyes, thick dark eyeliner, painted curly dark lashes, mauve blushed eye shadow, feathered brows, accented eye corners and nostrils, closed mouth with outlined lips, pierced ears, blonde mohair wig over cork pate, French kid bébé body with gusset-jointing at hips and knees, bisque lower arms with curled fingers. Condition: generally excellent. Marks: A. 5 T. (head and shoulder plate). Comments: Andre Thuillier, circa 1880, his earliest model bébé with superb definition of features, very lovely bisque with exceptional decoration around the eyes, original sturdy body, early woolen and velvet costume and bonnet, undergarments, leather shoes signed "A.T." $35,000/45,000

224. German Wooden Doll Furniture Attributed to Wagner & Sohne in Original Box

16" (41 cm.) x 10" box. 6"l. settee. A heavy board box with red paper cover contains a nine-piece set of wooden doll furniture with ebony finish decorated with elaborate gilded designs, in the style known as Biedermeier. Included is a marble top desk, mirrored armoire, upholstered settee, and six dining chairs. Furniture excellent, the box is worn. Germany, attributed to G.H. Wagner & Sohne, circa 1880. $800/1100

225. American Patented Walking Doll "Autoperipatetikous" by Martin & Runyan

11" (28 cm.) A paper-mache headed doll with beautifully sculpted detail of curly hair, painted facial features is mounted on original body with carton torso, leather arms, skirt-shaped lower torso containing clockwork mechanism, brass feet, antique cotton gown and petticoat. When wound, the doll slowly "walks" along on her little brass boot-shaped feet. Condition: generally excellent, mechanism functions, original painting albeit few minor craze lines on shoulder plate. Marks: (remains of original stamp on base). Comments: Martin & Runyan, circa 1868. Value Points: the rare early patented doll is preserved in her original box with illustration and directions for use, having especially fine detail of facial painting. $1200/1800

226. Large Early English Bookcase with Writing Desk

47" (119 cm.) h. x 26"w. x 14"d. The fine mahogany veneered bookcase with glass top windows opening to 2 shelved interior is fitted with cast bronze hardware and trim, and has a hidden pull-out writing surface with leather top. The lower cabinet has double doors that hinge open to reveal two interior shelves. English, early 19th century. Excellent condition. $1500/2500

227. French Singing Bird in Gilded Cage Attributed to Bontems

19" (48 cm.) A wooden framed base with carved detail and gold leaf finish supports a metal bird cage with brass finial and carrying loop. Inside on a brass perch is a blue and green feathered bird. When wound, the bird flutters his wings and tail feathers, pivots from side to side, opens and closes his beak, and "sings" realistic bird sound. French, circa 1880, attributed to Bontems. Excellent condition. $4000/4000

228. Very Large French Paper Mache Poupée with Antique Costume

36" (91 cm.) Solid domed paper mache shoulder head with rounded facial modeling, black painted pate with stippled curls around the face, black enamel inset eyes, painted lashes and brows, accented nostrils, open mouth, two upper and two lower teeth, kid poupée body with shapely torso, gusset-jointed limbs, stitched and separated fingers. Condition: generally excellent. Comments: for the French market, circa 1860. Value Points: grand exhibition size poupée with lovely antique silk costume, bonnet, blue kidskin slippers. $2000/3000

229. Petite French Bisque Bébé Steiner, Figure A, in Original Au Nain Bleu Costume

11" (28 cm.) Bisque socket head, blue glass paperweight inset eyes, painted lashes, brush-stroked brows, accented nostrils and eye corners, rose blushed eye shadow, thick brush-stroked brows, closed mouth with accented lips, pierced ears, blonde mohair wig over Steiner pate, Steiner composition and wooden fully-jointed body. Condition: generally excellent. Marks: A 3 (incised) Le Petit Parisien Bébé Steiner (body). Comments: Jules Steiner, circa 1895. Value Points: beautiful complexion and painting on the petite bébé, original body and body finish, wearing lovely antique costume that, although unsigned, is indubitably from the prestige workshops of Paris doll shop Au Nain Bleu. $3000/4000

230. French Bisque Waltzing Lady by Jules Steiner with Original London Toy Store Label

15" (38 cm.) Bisque swivel head on kid-edged bisque shoulder plate, blue glass enamel inset eyes, painted lashes, dark eyeliner, rose blushed eye shadow, brush-stroked brows, accented eye corners and nostrils, slightly parted lips, two rows of tiny teeth, pierced ears, brunette mohair wig over Steiner pate, kid-over-firm-carton torso, metal upper arms, bisque forearms, cone-shaped lower body/legs "skirt" which covers clockwork mechanism that is wound by attached brass key at the back, antique dress is included. Condition: generally excellent, mechanism functions well. Marks: Cremer Regent St. London Toys, Dolls, Games (original paper label on base). Comments: Jules Steiner, circa 1880, his deposed waltzing lady who glides forward, turns, twirls, pauses, glides again, when wound, originally sold by the prestige London toy store of Cremer. Value Points: especially pretty face on the well-functioning waltzing lady. $4000/6000

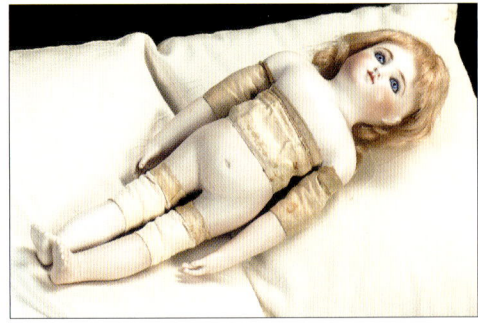

231. Very Rare French Bisque Taufling Baby by Jules Steiner

13" (33 cm.) Solid domed bisque shoulder head with sculpted upper arms, blue glass enamel inset eyes, painted curly lashes, rose blushed eye shadow, feathered brows, accented nostrils, closed mouth with accented lips, blonde mohair wig, twill upper arms, midriff, and upper legs, bisque lower arms, lower torso and hips, and lower legs with bare feet. Condition: generally excellent. Comments: Jules Steiner, his first bébé model, circa 1870, inspired by the Japanese Ichimatsu play doll introduced to Western culture at the mid-19th century International Expositions. Value Points: very rare early doll is enhanced by choicest bisque and painting, all original body parts, included is silk dress. $3500/5500

232. Outstanding French Bisque Bébé Steiner, Figure C in Grand 35" Size, with Bisque Hands

35" (89 cm.) Bisque socket head with plumply modeled cheeks, blue glass sleep eyes, dark eyeliner, rose blushed eye shadow, dark painted lashes, brush-stroked and feathered brows, accented eye corners, shaded nostrils, closed mouth with defined space between the shaded lips, pierced ears, blonde mohair wig over Steiner pate, French composition fully-jointed body with bisque hands, wearing lovely silk costume with lace overlay, velvet bonnet, undergarments, leather shoes, stockings. Condition: generally excellent, two fingers reglued. Marks: Figure C. No 7 Steiner Bte SGDG paris (head) Le Petit Parisien Bte SGDG (body). J. Steiner (eyes). Comments: Jules Steiner, circa 1884. Value Points: exceptional size of the rare early model allowing for wonderful expression, enhanced by choicest bisque and painting, very rare bisque hands with separately sculpted fingers, original body and body finish, lovely antique costume. $15,000/21,000

233. Tulle Fashion Gown with Handmade Lace Trim
To fit 15"-16" poupée. Of finely woven sheer tulle or net, the gown features a fitted bodice and widely flared skirt with flat front and gathered back, trimmed with bands of ivory silk satin ribbons and handmade looped lace at the neckline and sleeves. Excellent condition. Circa 1865. $600/900

234. French Bone-Handled Cream Parasol for Poupée in Original Box
7.5" (19 cm.) Having carved bone handle, the ivory silk satin covered parasol has long silk fringe and is preserved in its original box with boutique label of "Lemonnon, Blanchon Succ, Depot de Poupées Articulees, Lyon". Excellent condition. Circa 1870. $500/700

235. French Purple Silk Parasol for Poupée
7.5" (19 cm.) Having a carved bone handle with very rich silk cover in midnight purple with ivory silk fringe, the parasol is preserved in its original box. Excellent condition. French, circa 1870. $500/700

236. French Poupée's Feathered Muff in Original Box
3.5" (9 cm.) Beautifully constructed of alternate bands of soft white feathers and brown/black feathers, the silk-lined muff is preserved in its original green cylindrical box. French, circa 1870. Excellent condition. $400/500

237. Rare Early French Poupée's Sac du Voyage with Hand-Printed Muslin Cover
4.5" (11 cm.) The classic style sac du voyage has rectangular-shaped firm base with paper cover decorated with soft kidskin straps and brass studs that hinges open to lower compartment; with fabric upper compartment that opens at hinged clasp, woven braid leather handles. The fabric cover is early hand-woven muslin with transfer printed designs. An early penknife in the shape of woman's shoe is contained in the bottom compartment. French, circa 1850. Excellent condition. $1200/1800

238. Silk Costume for Poupée
To fit 16" poupée of the 1875 era. Of rich magenta silk the two piece ensemble features an intricately constructed skirt with modified bustle back, and is trimmed in ivory silk satin with lace collar and edging trimmed with paillettes. Excellent condition, partially re-made. Circa 1875. $300/500

239. Grand Rosewood Vitrine with Curved Glass Door and Silk Interior
28" (71 cm.) The wooden vitrine with beautifully grained and matched rosewood veneers has gracefully curved front wooden and glass panels, and a fitted interior of tufted silk in rich magenta color. Excellent condition, one rub to finish below door. Late 19th century. $800/1200

240. Gorgeous French Bisque Bébé E.J., Size 12, with Original Jumeau Couturier Costume
26" (66 cm.) Pressed bisque socket head, large amber brown glass paperweight inset eyes, thick dark eyeliner, painted dark curly lashes, rose blushed eye shadow, brush-stroked

and multi-feathered brows, accented eye corners, shaded nostrils, closed mouth with defined space between the shaded and outlined lips, separately applied pierced ears, blonde mohair wig over pierced ears, French composition and wooden eight-loose-ball-jointed body with straight wrists. Condition: generally excellent. Marks: Depose E 12 J (and artist check marks). Comments: Emile Jumeau, circa 1885. Value Points: exceptional beauty of the large bébé with finest luminous bisque, original wig, pate, body, body finish, and wearing extraordinary original costume from Ernestine Jumeau couturier workshops including fabulous dress, lace bonnet, and leather shoes with gold lettering "Bébé Jumeau". $9500/13,500

241. Beautiful French Bisque Poupée with All-Wooden Articulated Body
18" (46 cm.) Bisque swivel head on kid-edged bisque shoulder plate, blue glass enamel inset eyes, dark eyeliner, painted lashes, arched feathered brows, accented nostrils and eye corners, closed mouth with outlined lips, pierced ears, brunette human hair over cork pate, all-wooden body with shapely torso, dowel-jointing at shoulders, elbows, wrists, hips and knees, pivot jointing at upper arms and upper legs. Condition: generally excellent. Marks: 4. Comments: circa 1870. Value Points: very beautiful face enhanced by wonderful sculpting of curvaceous wooden body, extra articulation at upper arms and legs, included is antique silk and velvet gown, wooden handled parasol, leather boots, straw bonnet. $4000/5500

242. French Black Leather Shoes for Bru Jne, Size 5
2.5" (6 cm.) Of soft black kidskin with ankle straps, silver buttons, black leather bow with oval silver buckle, tan sole impressed "Bru Jne Paris 5". Very good condition. French, circa 1880. $600/900

243. French Bisque Poupée by Jumeau with Brown Eyes
18" (46 cm.) Bisque swivel head on kid-edged bisque shoulder plate, large brown glass enamel inset eyes, painted lashes, feathered brows, accented nostrils and eye corners, closed mouth with center accent line, pierced ears, blonde mohair wig over cork pate, French kid gusset-jointed body with stitched and separated fingers, lovely silk costume in the antique style. Condition: generally excellent. marks: 6 (and artist checkmarks) Jumeau Medaille d'Or Paris (body). Comments: Jumeau, circa 1880. Value Points: dramatic large brown eyes lend a distinctive look, very sturdy and clean original sturdy body. $2200/2800

244. French Bisque Wooden Bodied Poupée with Trunk and Trousseau
17" (43 cm.) Bisque swivel head on kid-edged bisque shoulder plate, grey glass enamel inset eyes, dark eyeliner, painted curly lashes, arched feathered brows, accented nostrils and eye corners, closed mouth with center accent line, pierced ears, brunette mohair wig over cork pate, French all-wooden body with dowel jointing at shoulders, elbows, wrists, hips, knees and ankles, swivel waist, and pivot upper legs. Condition: generally excellent. Marks: 4 (head and shoulders). Comments: Gaultier, circa 1875. Value Points: superb detail of wooden body with deluxe articulation points, separately carved fingers, lovely bisque, along with her original French poupée trunk having original brass "articles de voyage" maker's label, and seven antique gowns, with various accessories. $6500/8500

245. Rare French Cast Iron Recamier for Poupée
20" (51 cm.) l. Of heavy cast iron with deeply sculpted designs, scrolled edging and feet, curved sides with metal rod frames, fitted with antique paisley pillows. French, circa 1870, possibly Coudreau, who was listed in La Poupée Modele as a maker of iron doll's beds for 17" poupées. The very rare bed is in excellent condition. $800/1300

246. French Leather Shoes for Bru Jne, Size 2
1.5" (4 cm.) Of soft black kidskin with brown overcast thread edging, ankle straps with silver buttons, black leather bows with round silver buckle, the shoes are impressed on the tan soles with "Bru Jne Paris 2". Excellent condition. Circa 1888. $400/600

247. Rare Collection of French Cloth "Poupées Fabrette"

16" (41 cm.) Ten stockinette softly stuffed fashion ladies, each with painted facial features and arranged wigs, wearing fashionable costume of a particular season, social occasion, or historical event. Several of the dolls are posed on original fabric covered stands and several have original paper label with ink script indicating the style of costume portrayed, viz. "Pendant la Guerre de 1914", "Les Entrapees 1910-1912", "Temps des Tournures, vers 1882", "Sous la Emire, 1805", "Entraree (?) 1910", "Les Entrapees 1910-1912", and "Mariee 1900". Condition: fair to excellent, mostly in fine original condition with well-preserved, albeit delicate, costume. Marks: Poupée Fabrette (on several). Comments: circa 1915, Paris. Value Points: rare fashion dolls in well-preserved condition with documentation labels. $800/1200

248. French Bisque Poupée by Gaultier in Original Folklore Costume of Normandy

15" (38 cm.) Bisque swivel head on kid-edged bisque shoulder plate, blue glass enamel inset eyes, dark eyeliner, painted lashes, lightly feathered brows, accented nostrils and eye corners, closed mouth with center accent line on lips, pierced ears, blonde mohair wig captured under coiffe, kid poupée body with gusset-jointing at elbows, hips and knees. Condition: generally excellent. Marks: 2. Comments: Gaultier, circa 1880. Value Points: the poupée wears her original folklore costume of Normandy including Alencon fiche and very elaborate bridal coiffe. $2000/3000

249. French Bisque Poupée with Rare Kid-over-Wooden Body Attributed to Arnaud

14" (36 cm.) Bisque shoulder head with pale complexion, plump facial features, cobalt blue glass enamel eyes, dark eyeliner, painted lashes and brows, accented nostrils, closed mouth with accented lips, unpierced ears, blonde human hair over cork pate, French poupée body of kid-stretched over wooden form, wooden arms with dowel-articulation at shoulders and elbows, cupped wooden hands, antique silk gown, undergarments, leather slippers. Condition: generally excellent, finish on hands worn. Comments: body style attributed to Arnaud, whose deposed patent drawings are shown in *The Encyclopedia of French Dolls* by Theimer, page 23. Value Points: beautiful bright-eyed poupée with rarer body. $3500/4500

250. French Bisque Poupée with Cobalt Blue Eyes

18" (46 cm.) Very pale bisque shoulder head with plump facial shape, cobalt blue glass enamel inset eyes, dark eyeliner, painted lashes and lightly feathered brows, accented nostrils, closed mouth with accented lips, blushed cheeks and chin, unpierced ears, blonde mohair wig over cork pate, kid poupée body with shapely torso, gusset-jointing at elbows, hips and knees, stitched and separated fingers. Condition: generally excellent. Comments: in the Barrois style, circa 1860. Value Points: brilliant eyes are a beautiful contrast to delicate bisque, sturdy body, original wig, lovely antique brown silk taffeta gow, lace bonnet, undergarments, very fancy leather boots. $2500/3000

251. Pair, French Paper Mache Characters "Toto" and "Tata" by Roullet et Decamps

14" (36 cm.) Each has paper mache head with characterized expression, painted smiling closed mouth, upturned nose, he with blue glass eyes and bisque hands, she with painted blue eyes and paper mache hands, brunette human hair, carton torso with mechanism, paper mache legs hinge-attached to torso. Condition: generally excellent, boy's mechanism functions well, girl needs adjustment. Comments: Roullet et Decamps, circa 1910, the dolls were modeled after drawings of Montmartre urchins by French artist Poulbot for Decamps, named "Toto" and "Tata". Value Points: delightful characters, the boy especially pleasing with glass eyes, turning head, tilting side to side. $2000/3000

252. French Bisque Bébé with Character Expression by Joanny

22" (56 cm.) Bisque socket head, plumply modeled cheeks, large blue glass paperweight inset eyes, dark eyeliner, dark painted lashes, rose blushed eye shadow, brush-stroked and multi-feathered brows, accented nostrils and eye corners, closed mouth with defined space between the outlined lips, pierced ears, brunette human hair, French composition and wooden fully-jointed body. Condition: generally excellent, head and body not original to each other but appropriately sized and styled and of the same era. Marks: J - 10 (incised, head) Jumeau Medaille d'Or Paris (body). Comments: Joanny, circa 1890. Value Points: rarely found model with appealing character expression, fine quality of painting, antique mariner costume. $4500/6500

253. French Bisque Character Man by Defuisseux

11" (28 cm.) Bisque socket head of adult man with darkened unshaven complexion, painted facial features, brown eyes, red and black upper eyeliner, thick brows, large pointy nose, closed mouth with grim expression, grey mohair wig, composition and wooden ball-jointed body,

grey woolen suit, shirt, shoes. Condition: generally excellent. Marks: D.F./B B3. Comments: Defuisseaux, circa 1910. Value Points: rare model with exceptional quality of artistic and highly characterized painting. $800/1000

254. Rare Grand-size French Bisque Pouting Character, 252, by SFBJ
26" (66 cm.) Bisque socket head with very plump cheeks, small blue glass sleep eyes, mohair lashes, fringe-painted lashes, short feathered brows, accented nostrils and eye corners, rounded nose, closed mouth with very full pouting lips, brunette mohair wig, French composition and wooden fully-jointed toddler body with side-hip jointing, antique costume. Condition: generally excellent. Marks: SFBJ 252 Paris 11 (head) SFBJ (torso label). Comments: SFBJ, circa 1910. Value Points: wonderful large size of the rarer model from their art character series, the large size allowing superb definition of facial features, finest quality of bisque, original toddler body with original finish. $4500/6500

255. French Mechanical Knitting Bunny by Roullet & Decamps
12" (30 cm.) Paper mache bunny is lavishly covered with white fur, has amber glass eyes, floppy ears, and is posed standing, holding knitting work in its hands. When wound, the bunny should vigorously move arms up and down, turning head, as though knitting. Condition: structurally excellent, mechanism needs review. Marks: R.D. (key). Comments: Roullet et Decamps, circa 1900. Value Points: amusing automaton with well-preserved structure, fur, and accessories. $900/1300

256. German Bisque Child, 908, by Simon and Halbig
16" (41 cm.) Bisque socket head, brown glass inset eyes, dark eyeliner, painted short lashes and feathered brows, accented nostrils and eye corners, slightly parted lips with two square-cut teeth, pierced ears, auburn mohair wig, composition and wooden ball-jointed body, red silk antique style costume. Condition: generally excellent, some body retouch. Marks: S 7 H 908. Comments: Simon and Halbig, circa 1885. Value Points: rare early Simon and Halbig model with appealing expression and lovely bisque. $2000/2500

257. German Mechanical Toy "Milkmaid and the Moo-ing Cow", Possibly Zinner and Sohne
11" (28 cm.) l. 11" h. overall. Posed upon a wooden box-shaped platform with four red spoked wheels is a bisque-headed doll with brown glass inset eyes, painted lashes and brows, accented nostrils, closed mouth, pierced ears, blonde human hair, carton torso and shapely legs, wire upper arms, paper mache lower arms, alongside a flocked-finish paper mache brown cow with horns, udder and large painted eyes, and a feeding trough and wooden bucket. When the toy is pulled along, the girl briskly moves forward and back as though urging the cow home, the cow turns its head from side to side, moo's, and flicks its tail in an amusing manner. Condition: generally excellent. Marks: 802 o. Comments: circa 1885, doll's head by Simon and Halbig, the intricate mechanism is visible beneath the platform. Value Points: delightful automaton with amusing action, original milkmaid costume, especially beautiful doll face. $3500/5500

258. Rare German Brown-Complexioned Bisque Character, 1358, by Simon and Halbig
16" (41 cm.) Bisque socket head with brown-complexion, brown glass sleep eyes, black brush-stroked brows with feathered highlights, accented nostrils and eye corners, rounded nose, open mouth with full coral-shaded lips, four porcelain teeth, pierced ears, black human hair, brown composition and wooden ball-jointed body, wearing

259. Set, All-Bisque Miniature Dolls in Original Costumes and Presentation Box
2.5" (6 cm.) Each is all-bisque miniature with swivel head, painted facial features, mohair wig, peg-jointed bisque arms and legs with painted black shoes. Condition: generally excellent. Comments: for the French market, circa 1890. Value Points: the set of miniature dolls wear their factory original costumes and are presented in original store box with illustrations of children on the cover. $800/1000

260. Rare and Beautiful German Brown-Complexioned Bisque Doll Known as "A.T. Kestner"
12" (30 cm.) Bisque socket head with cafe-au-lait complexion, brown glass sleep eyes, black painted lashes and brows, accented nostrils, closed mouth with coral-shaded lips, pierced ears, black mohair wig, early composition and wooden fully-jointed body with straight wrists, wearing original factory chemise, shoes and socks, another dress included. Condition: generally excellent, pierced ear holes pulled through, arms repainted. Marks: 7. Comments: Kestner, circa 1884, the model closely resembles the French bébé by Thuillier marked A.T. Value Points: very rare model with entrancing expression and very beautiful quality of bisque and complexion. $3500/5500

lovely silk dress, straw bonnet, undergarments, shoes. Condition: generally excellent. Marks: 1358 Germany Simon & Halbig S&H 4. Comments: circa 1910, Simon and Halbig. Value Points: rare model with very beautiful rich complexion flawlessly preserved, original body and body finish. $4500/6500

261. Very Fine French Bisque Bébé Brevete by Leon Casimir Bru
21" (53 cm.) Pressed bisque swivel head on kid-edged bisque shoulder plate, plump facial modeling, blue glass enamel inset eyes with spiral threading, dark eyeliner, painted lashes, mauve blushed eye shadow, feathered brows, accented eye corners, shaded nostrils, closed mouth with defined space between the outlined lips, pierced ears, blonde fleecy lambswool wig over cork pate, French kid bébé body with square cut collarette, gusset-jointed limbs, bisque lower arms and hands. Condition: generally excellent. Comments: Leon Casimir Bru, his "brevete" first model bébé, circa 1877. Value Points: exceptional beauty of the earliest model bébé with dramatic eyes, subtle painting of blushed details, original wig, original very sturdy body, antique cashmere cream woolen coat

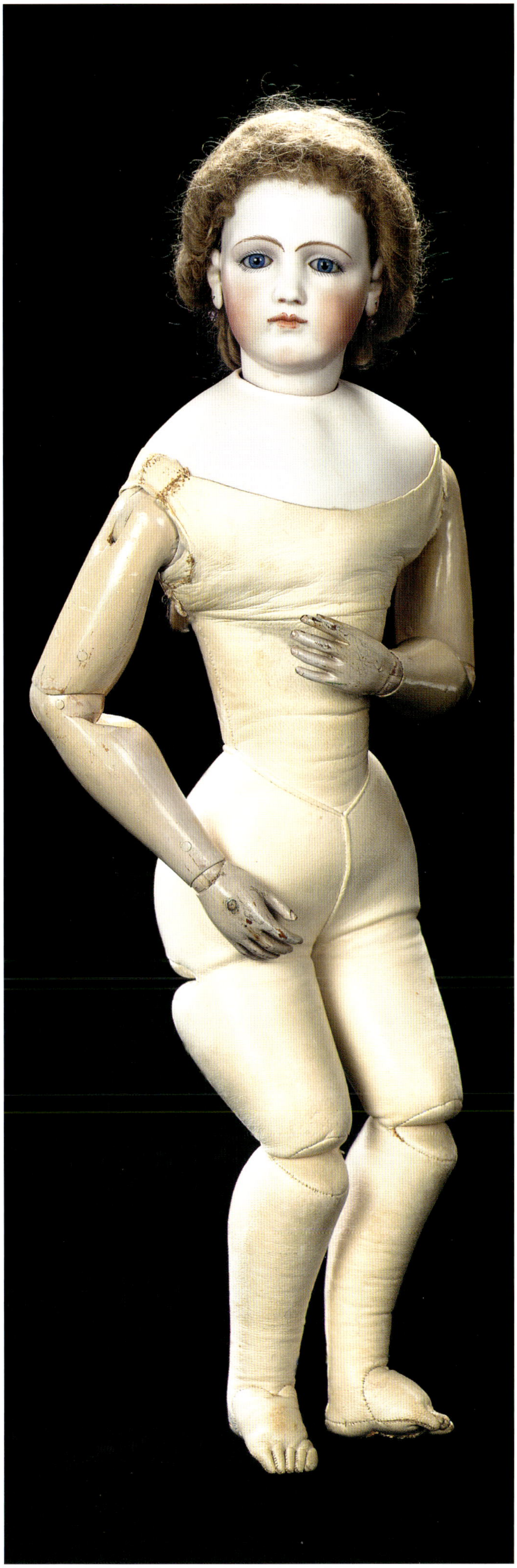

dress with capelet collar, straw bonnet, undergarments, leather shoes with silk rosettes. $17,000/25,000

262. Beautiful French Bisque Portrait Bébé by Jumeau
19" (48 cm.) Pressed bisque socket head, large blue glass enamel inset eyes, dark eyeliner, rose blushed eye shadow, lightly feathered brows, accented nostrils and eye corners, closed mouth with outlined lips, pierced ears, blonde mohair wig over cork pate, French composition and wooden eight-loose-ball-jointed body with straight wrists. Condition: generally excellent. Marks: 2 (head) Jumeau Medaille d'Or Paris (body). Comments: Emile Jumeau, circa 1878, his first period portrait model bébé. Value Points: gorgeous face enhanced by very beautiful painting with subtle blushing, lovely antique costume, bonnet, undergarments, leather shoes. $5500/7500

263. Gorgeous French Bisque Poupée by Pierre-Francois Jumeau with Wooden Arms
22" (56 cm.) Pressed bisque swivel head on kid-edged bisque shoulder plate, very full cheeks, narrow almond shaped blue glass enamel inset eyes, dark eyeliner, painted lashes, mauve blushed eye shadow, arched feathered brows, accented nostrils and eye corners, closed mouth with shaded and accented lips, blushed dimpled chin, separately modeled applied ears, brunette mohair wig over cork pate, French kid poupée body with gusset-jointing at hips and knees, wooden arms with dowel jointing at shoulders, elbows and wrists, separately sculpted fingers, ivory satin costume in the antique style is included. Condition: generally excellent. Comments: Pierre-Francois Jumeau, circa 1870. Value Points: exceptional beauty of the larger poupée with finest quality of bisque, rarer body style. $5000/7500

127

264. Lovely French Bisque Bébé by Schmitt & Fils with Original Lambswool Wig

19" (48 cm.) Pressed bisque socket head, deep blue glass paperweight inset eyes, dark eyeliner, painted lashes, brush-stroked and multi-feathered brows, mauve blushed eye shadow, accented eye corners, shaded nostrils, closed mouth with defined space between the outlined lips, pierced ears, blonde lambswool wig over cork pate, French composition and wooden eight-loose-ball-jointed body with straight wrists. Condition: generally excellent. Marks: Sch (in shield, head and derriere). Comments: Schmitt et Fils, circa 1884. Value Points: beautiful bébé with highly defined facial features, especially beautiful quality of bisque, original wig, body, body finish, lovely antique costume. $9000/13,000

265. French Wooden Doll Size Bedroom Furniture

13" (33 cm.) h. chair. Of pinewood with original creamy white painted finish, the bedroom ensemble comprises a bed with fittings, cane-seated chair and a marbletop night stand. Each is embellished with bronze decorative garlands or wreaths. Excellent condition. French, circa 1885, appropriately sized for display with dolls about 18"-20". $800/1200

266. Collection of 19th Century Porcelain Inkwells and Trinket Boxes

5". Six porcelain figurals depicting children or homelike settings include three inkwells and three trinket boxes; of particular interest is a fine porcelain polychrome figure of child hugging a bunny which, when lid is removed, reveals a double inkwell. Excellent condition, few small chips. Mid-19th century. $800/1000

267. Very Rare Grand-Sized French Bisque Bébé, Series C, by Jules Steiner

37" (94 cm.) Bisque socket head, blue glass paperweight inset eyes, dark eyeliner, painted lashes, mauve blushed eye shadow, brush-stroked and feathered brows, accented eye corners, shaded nostrils, closed mouth with outlined lips, pierced ears, blonde human hair over original Steiner pate, Steiner composition and wooden fully-jointed body. Condition: generally excellent. Marks: Sie C (incised) J. Steiner Bte SGDG Bourgoin (red ink script). Comments: Jules Steiner, Series C, circa 1884. Value Points: very rare exhibition size model of the wistful-faced child with superlative quality of bisque, modeling and painting, original body and body finish, beautiful antique pique costume, straw bonnet, shoes, undergarments; few examples of this size model are known to exist. $15,000/20,000

268. French Bisque Portrait Bébé by Jumeau with Rare Expression
22" (56 cm.) Pressed bisque socket head, very deep blue glass paperweight inset eyes, thick dark eyeliner, painted curly lashes, mauve blushed eye shadow, arched feathered brows, accented eye corners and nostrils, closed mouth with defined space between the outlined lips, separately applied pierced ears, blonde mohair wig over cork pate, French composition and wooden eight-loose-ball-jointed body with straight wrists, beautifully costumed in blue velvet coat dress with lace collar, lace dress, undergarments, blue velvet bonnet, leather shoes. Condition: generally excellent. Marks: 10 (head) Jumeau Medaille d'Or Paris (body). Comments: Emile Jumeau, circa 1882. Value Points: fine modeling enhanced by luminous bisque with nicely blushed details, spectacular eyes, acquired from the Mildred Seeley Collection by Geri Baker. $7500/9500

269. French Doll's Chair with Blue Silk Tufted Seat
16" (41 cm.) Faux-bamboo bentwood chair with elegant looped design back and arms is upholstered in tufted ice blue silk. Excellent condition. French, circa 1890. $300/500

270. French Bisque Poupée by Jumeau in Superb Original Turkish Exhibition Costume
14" (36 cm.) Bisque swivel head on kid-edged bisque shoulder plate, large blue glass enamel inset eyes, dark painted lashes, feathered brows, accented nostrils, closed mouth with accented lips, pierced ears, blonde mohair wig over cork pate, French kid poupée body with shapely torso. Condition: generally excellent. Marks: 4. Comments: Emile Jumeau, circa 1878, the poupée was likely prepared as an exhibition model for an international exposition as indicated by both the high quality of the facial sculpture and detail, and the extraordinary original and authentic costume designed to appeal to international traveling royalty. Value Points: the elaborate original costume of fine silks, lace and embroidery with elaborate coiffe is perfectly preserved, the body is near mint, the bisque flawless. $4000/6000

271. Petite French Bisque Poupée with Lovely Antique Costume
14" (36 cm.) Bisque swivel head on kid-edged bisque shoulder plate, cobalt blue glass enamel inset eyes, painted lashes, multi-feathered brows, accented eye corners and nostrils, closed mouth with center accent line, blushed cheeks, ears pierced into head, brunette mohair wig over cork pate, French kid gusset-jointed body with stitched and separated fingers. Condition: generally excellent. Marks: 1 (head and shoulders). Comments: circa 1875. Value Points: very appealing expression with pert features, lovely bisque, dramatic blue eyes, pretty antique two piece gown, undergarments, leather boots. $1700/2500

272. French Bisque Smiling Poupée by Leon Casimir Bru
16" (41 cm.) Bisque swivel head on kid-lined bisque shoulder plate, pale blue glass enamel inset eyes, dark eyeliner, painted lashes, arched feathered brows, accented nostrils and eye corners, closed mouth with accented lips, pierced ears, blonde mohair wig over cork pate, kid poupée body with gusset-jointing at hips, knees, and elbows, stitched and separated fingers, nicely bostumed in antique frock, undergarments, lace bonnet, leather shoes. Condition: generally excellent. Marks: E. Comments: Leon Casimir Bru, circa 1872, his deposed poupée model with smiling expression. Value Points: lovely refined lady with gentle smile, fine quality of bisque and painting. $2500/3500

273. Rare Early French "Elise's Poupée" with Extensive Early Trousseau

15" (38 cm.) Solid domed carton shoulder head with painted facial features, blue down-glancing eyes, single stroke brows and upper eye liner, closed mouth with accent line between the lips, tacked-on brunette wig, original very slender kid hand-stitched body with high waist, wooden "griffe" hands. Condition: generally excellent, some early repaint of complexion is possible, body very sturdy and clean. Comments: French, circa 1840. Value Points: rare early doll with fine original body and wig, her trousseau of the 1830/40 era, comprises four dresses, extensive undergarments including stylized muslin back hoop, four bonnets, collar, chemisettes, and a silk pillow with tiny silver lettering "Poupée d'Elise". $1200/1800

274. German Paper Mache Lady with Ornate Coiffure

16" (41 cm.) Paper mache shoulder head of adult lady with oval face and elongated strong throat, black sculpted hair waved in front of ears and smoothed backward into ringlet curl behind each ear and tightly coiled chignon at the back of head, painted facial features, blue eyes, red and black eyeliner, slender kid body with wooden lower limbs, painted orange shoes. Condition: generally excellent, slight nose rub, horizontal craze at back shoulder plate. Comments: Germany, circa 1840. Value Points: fine larger size of the early poupée with beautiful hair styling, sturdy original body $800/1200

275. American Paper Mache Doll by Ludwig Greiner

23" (58 cm.) Paper mache shoulder head with rounded childlike shape, sculpted black hair in short finger curls tucked behind the ears, painted blue upper glancing eyes, red and black eyeliner, single stroke brows, accented nostrils, closed mouth with center accent line, muslin stitch-jointed body, antique gown, undergarments, apron, red kidskin slippers. Condition: generally excellent. Comments: attributed to Ludwig Greiner, circa 1880. Value Points: very appealing facial expression, beautiful original finish. $600/900

276. German Paper Mache Lady Doll with Long Black Sculpted Curls
10" (25 cm.) Paper mache shoulder head with slender oval face and elongated throat, black sculpted hair in long ringlet curls that fall onto her shoulders, painted facial features, azure blue eyes, black upper eyeliner and brows, accented nostrils, closed mouth, slender kid body

with wooden lower limbs, painted shoes. Condition: generally excellent. Comments: Germany, circa 1850. Value Points: the well-preserved doll has original finish, wearing original costume, and presented on velvet covered wooden stand. $600/900

277. German Paper Mache Doll with Brown Eyes in Original Costume
9" (23 cm.) Paper mache shoulder head with black sculpted hair arranged in short finger curls, painted facial features, brown eyes, black brows and eyeliner, accented nostrils, closed mouth with pertly shaped lips, slender kid body, wooden lower limbs, painted green shoes, antique costume. Condition: generally excellent. Comments: Germany, circa 1860. Value Points: beautiful original complexion and painting, rarer brown eyes. $400/600

278. German Paper Mache Child with Sculpted Hair and Glass Eyes
25" (64 cm.) Paper mache shoulder head with rounded childlike facial shape, sculpted short curly hair with stippled detailing, black enamel inset eyes, painted lashes, lightly feathered brows, accented nostrils and eye corners, closed mouth with center accent line, sculpted ears, muslin stitch-jointed body, leather arms. Condition: very good, original finish with some typical craze lines. Comments: Germany, circa 1880. Value Points: especially fine detail of sculpted curly hair, original body, wearing wonderful antique dress with attached linen bodice and cuffs, undergarments, leather boots. $1100/1500

279. Four Miniature Grodnertal Wooden "Tuck Comb" Dolls in Original Costumes

4" (10 cm.) Each has one piece carved wooden head and torso, peg-jointed wooden arms and legs, painted black hair with defined yellow comb at the crest, painted complexion over gesso, painted facial features, wearing original multi-layered gowns. Also included is a tiny wooden walnut cradle containing tiny Grodnertal (without legs) in baby gown. Excellent condition. Circa 1840. $1000/1300

280. Ten Wonderful German Miniature Grodnertal Dolls in Original Costumes

4" (10 cm.) Each is all wooden with one piece head and torso, jointed limbs at shoulders, elbows, hips and knees, painted hair and facial features, painted shoes. Condition: generally excellent. Comments: Grodnertal, circa 1840. Value Points: superb preservation of the early miniature dolls with wonderful costumes representing various people such as nanny holding baby, little boy with drum, lady with sculpted ornate hair, velvet suited boy with hat in hand, Marquis with silk costume and bi-corn hat. $1200/1800

281. German Miniature All-Wooden Doll in Chaise a Porteur

4" (10 cm.) doll. 4 1/2" chaise a porteur. An all-wooden doll with one-piece head and torso, painted black hair, painted complexion and facial features, has peg-jointed body at shoulders, elbows, hips and knees and painted flat orange shoes, wearing original costume and coiffe. The doll is seated in a tapestry-covered wooden chaise a porteur with curved top roof, opening glass door, carrying bars, and silk and velvet lining. Excellent condition. Ex-collection Legoland Museum of Antique Dolls before acquisition by Geri Baker. Circa 1850. $500/800

282. Two Miniature Grodnertal Dolls in Coronation Robes
3.5" (9 cm.) Each is all-wooden doll with one piece head and shapely torso, black painted hair and facial features, jointed shoulders, elbows, hips and knees, painted lower legs and flat shoes, Condition: very good, finish on hair well worn. Comments: Grodnertal, circa 1850. Value Points: representing Queen Victoria and Albert at her coronation, wearing their purple velvet coronation robe with faux-ermine trim, and each with its own velvet covered wooden kneeling prie-dieu. $400/600

283. German Paper Mache Doll in Original Folklore Costume
11" (28 cm.) Solid domed paper mache shoulder head with black enamel eyes, painted features, black painted pate, closed mouth, hand-stitched kid body with stitched and separated fingers. Condition: generally excellent. Comments: circa 1865. Value Points: the doll wears elaborate original folklore costume and beaded head-dress, an original paper label reads "costume doll, Central European late 18th century". $400/500

284. 19th Century Neopolitan Woman in Original Costume
20" (51 cm.) Terra cotta shoulder head portraying a woman with long sculpted grey hair in tousled style, deeply defined facial features with age wrinkles, enamel eyes, strong nose, closed mouth with defined teeth, definition of throat muscles, hemp-wrapped armature body, terra cotta sculpted hands and feet in very expressive poses. Condition: generally excellent, one baby finger broken, original finish with very minor wear. Comments: Neopolitan, early 19th century. Value Points: fine large size with beautiful sculpting, original elaborate silk costume of village lady, the costume lined with old Italian papers. $700/1000

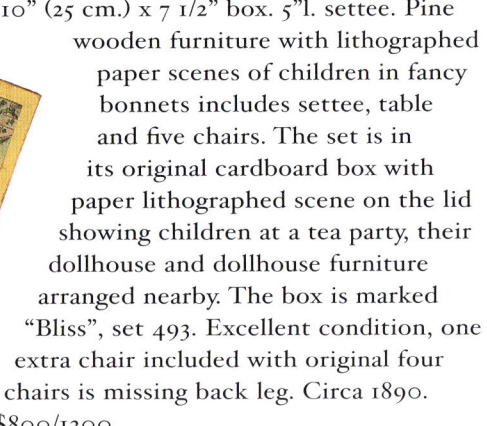

285. American Wooden "Parlor Furniture" by Bliss in Original Box

10" (25 cm.) x 7 1/2" box. 5"l. settee. Pine wooden furniture with lithographed paper scenes of children in fancy bonnets includes settee, table and five chairs. The set is in its original cardboard box with paper lithographed scene on the lid showing children at a tea party, their dollhouse and dollhouse furniture arranged nearby. The box is marked "Bliss", set 493. Excellent condition, one extra chair included with original four chairs is missing back leg. Circa 1890. $800/1200

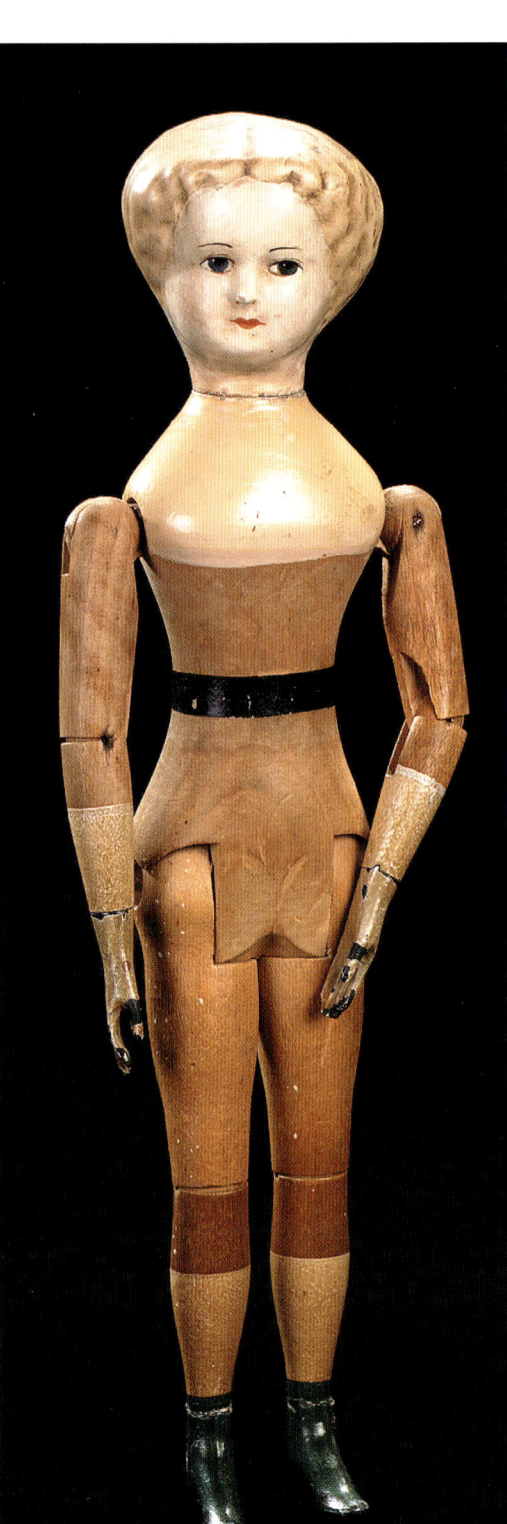

286. American Wooden Doll by Mason-Taylor with Original Finish

12" (30 cm.) All wooden doll has swivel head with painted and sculpted hair and facial features over gesso undercoat, short blonde sculpted curls, blue eyes with unusual side-glancing expression, painted brows and upper eyeliner, closed mouth with center accent line, shapely torso with black paper belt, dowel jointing at shoulders, elbows, hips and knees, metal hands and feet, painted blue ankle boots, antique costume included. Condition: generally excellent. Comments: Mason-Taylor, circa 1880. Value Points: fine original condition of the early American doll. $800/1100

287. American Wooden Doll House by Bliss

17" (43 cm.) Wooden two story doll house has paper lithographed cover which simulates the exterior shingles, curtained windows, second floor balcony, first floor porch columns, and over the opening front door. The paper lithography extends to the sides of the house and shingled steeple roof. The entire front hinges open to reveal two large interior rooms. The name Bliss is printed on the balcony trim. Good condition, some paper fading and spotting. Circa 1890. $800/1200

288. American Wooden Circus by Schoenhut in Original Box

19" (48 cm.) x 14" box. A red cardboard box with colorful drawing on the lid depicting the circus set, interior lid photographs showing play possibilities, and contains the following animals, people and accessories: two clowns with applied faces and original costumes, bisque-head acrobat lady with original costume, elephant, dappled horse with balancing stand, cloth ruff poodle, brown donkey, goat with goatee, horns and ears, two chairs, two ladders, 4 barrels and stands, along with an early Schoenhut catalog, and homemade programs and tickets made by the German children who played with circus. All the animals are glass-eyed. Condition: generally excellent, minor play wear. Comments: Schoenhut, circa 1910. Value Points: fine original condition, original box and catalog. $1500/2000

289. American Wooden Girl with Pink Hair Ribbon by Schoenhut

14" (36 cm.) Carved wooden socket head, carved hair in short bobbed fashion with defined bangs, sculpted and painted hair band terminating in bow at the back of the head, sculpted facial features, intaglio eyes, white upper glancing eyes, feathered brows, accented nostrils, closed mouth with pouting expression, all-wooden spring-jointed body with holes in feet for positioning. Condition: generally excellent. Marks: Schoenhut Doll Jat. Jan 17 '11, USA and Foreign Countries. Comments: Schoenhut,

circa 1912. Value Points: superb detail of carving enhanced by original finish depicts a very wistful child, rare hair style, original knit teddy and Schoenhut stand. $1000/1300

290. American Cloth Doll with Sculpted Bobbed Hair by Martha Chase

15" (38 cm.) All cloth doll with pressed and oil painted facial features, sculpted blonde hair in short bobbed fashion with bangs, blue upper glancing eyes, red and black upper eyeliner, upper fringed lashes, white eyedots, blonde brows, accented nostrils of upturned nose, closed mouth, stitch-jointing of shoulders, elbows, hips and knees, wearing pretty cotton dress. Condition: generally excellent, retouch to paint on limbs. Marks: (Chase Dutch girl logo on torso). Comments: Martha Chase, circa 1910. Value Points: especially pretty face with rosy cheeks, fine original painting of hair and face. $800/1000

291. Native American Cloth Doll with Leather Face and Original Costume

25" (64 cm.) Very slender oval face of soft kidskin that is treated for a canvas like effect, shaped nose and lips, brown oil painted complexion, large upper glancing outlined eyes, painted lips and teeth, black horsehair stitched hair, muslin body with padded armature arms for posing. Condition: generally excellent, some fading of original costume. Comments: Native American play doll, 19th century. Value Points: very rare doll in well-preserved original condition, wearing original handmade cotton dress, muslin apron, shawl, head scarf, black stockings, kidskin moccasins. The doll is shown in the book, *More Dolls, The Early Years* by Florence Theriault. $800/1200

292. American Wooden Doll Carriage in the Joel Ellis Manner

30" (76 cm.) Gracefully curved wooden carriage bed in unusual style allowing a seat for passenger and another for front "driver", is painted original royal blue with gold and brown stenciling, has four wooden yellow spoked wheels, and natural wood handle. Very good condition, original paint with some rubs. American, circa 1875. $600/900

293. Sonneberg Bisque Doll with Lovely Pale Complexion
18" (46 cm.) Pale bisque socket head with flattened solid dome, brilliant blue glass enamel inset eyes, dark eyeliner, delicately painted lashes, feathered brows, accented nostrils and eye corners, closed mouth with defined space between the outlined lips, blonde mohair wig, French composition and wooden fully-jointed body, moss green and bronze silk satin dress, undergarments, brown stockings, leather shoes, brown velvet bonnet. Condition: generally excellent, body not original but of the period and appropriately sized. Marks: 12 (head) Bébé Jumeau Diplome d'Honneur (body stamp). Comments: Sonneberg, mystery maker, circa 1885, the doll was made to emulate and capture the French doll market. Value Points: very beautiful pale bisque with brilliantly contrasting blue eyes. $1200/1800

294. German Bisque Doll, 949, by Simon and Halbig in Original Nun's Habit
13" (33 cm.) Bisque swivel head on kid-lined bisque shoulder plate, bright blue glass inset eyes, painted dark lashes, brush-stroked brows, accented nostrils and eye corners, closed mouth with center accent line, commercial pink muslin stitch-jointed body, bisque lower arms. Condition: generally excellent. Marks: SH 3 949. Comments: Simon and Halbig, circa 1885. Value Points: very beautiful swivel head, closed mouth doll, wearing her original brown woolen nun's habit with all appropriate accessories. $800/1200

295. German Bisque Lady Doll with Original Costume
15" (38 cm.) Solid domed bisque shoulder head with very plump face, pale bisque, painted bright blue eyes with glazed highlights, black eyeliner, painted lashes, lightly feathered brows, single stroke brows, accented nostrils and eye

corners, blonde mohair wig in waist-length braids, muslin stitch-jointed body, leather arms, stitched-on stockings and

blue kidskin boots, antique gown and undergarments. Condition: generally excellent. Comments: Germany, circa 1875. Value Points: very beautiful doll with unusually fine painting of eyes, original body and costume. $500/800

296. Two Petite German Bisque Portrait Dolls with Sculpted Hair
9.5" (24 cm.) Each has bisque shoulder head with oval facial modeling of adult lady, elongated throat, blonde sculpted hair, painted facial features, muslin body, bisque lower limbs, antique costume. Condition: generally excellent. Comments: Germany, circa 1870. Value Points: each with detailed sculpting, one having sculpted bodice and snood, the other with beautiful cheek color and brilliant blue eyes with tiny fringed lashes, along with molded purple lustre tasseled hair feather and green snood. $800/1000

plump cheeks, blonde sculpted boyish hair, blue glass eyes, painted lashes and brows, accented nostrils and eye corners, closed mouth with center accent line, kid body, composition hands. Condition: generally excellent. Marks: 6. Comments: attributed to Kling, circa 1875. Value Points: fine lustrous patina of bisque, glass eyes, wearing original folklore costume. $800/1100

298. German Bisque Doll, 166, by Kling
16" (41 cm.) Solid domed bisque shoulder head turned slightly to the right, brown glass eyes, painted lashes and brows, accented nostrils and eye corners, closed mouth with downcast lips, blonde mohair wig, muslin stitch-jointed body, composition lower legs, bisque arms from above the elbows, nicely costumed. Condition: generally excellent, one thumb chipped. Marks: 166-4. Comments: Kling, circa 1885. Value Points: very endearing wistful expression, fine bisque, body, and costume, ex-collection Legoland Museum of Antique Dolls before acquisition by Geri Baker. $800/1000

299. German Bisque Doll, 131, by Kling
12" (30 cm.) Bisque shoulder head with blonde sculpted hair in short curls and forehead bangs, brown glass inset eyes, painted lashes and brows, accented nostrils and eye corners, closed mouth with center accent line, muslin stitch-jointed body, bisque lower arms, antique costume. Condition: generally excellent, some finger tip chips. Marks: 131-3. Comments: Kling, circa 1880. Value Points: beautifully sculpted hair with deep comb-marks enhanced by decorative glaze, glass eyes. $400/500

297. German Bisque Glass-eyed Doll with Sculpted Hair in Original Costume
16" (41 cm.) Solid domed bisque shoulder head with rounded facial modeling,

300. German Bisque Doll with Sculpted Hair Known as Alice
10" (25 cm.) Bisque shoulder head with pale complexion, blonde sculpted hair waved away from face into short pageboy curls, sculpted hair band, painted facial features, bright blue eyes, red and black upper eyeliner, accented nostrils, closed mouth, muslin stitch-jointed body, bisque lower limbs, wearing muslin gown and undergarments. Condition: generally excellent. Comments: Germany, circa 1880. Value Points: beautiful original condition and costume of the petite early doll. $400/600

301. German Bisque Painted Eye Character by Kestner
18" (46 cm.) Bisque socket head, painted facial features, pale blue upper glancing eyes with white eyedots, black eyeliner with fringed lashes, red eyeliner, short feathered brows, accented nostrils and eye corners, closed mouth in smiling expression with row of beaded teeth, blonde mohair wig over plaster pate, composition and wooden ball-jointed body, wearing blue velvet Sunday best suit with lace collar, leather shoes, velvet cap. Condition: generally excellent. Comments: Kestner, circa 1912, the model appeared in a smaller version in their multi-head series. Value Points: rare larger size of the laughing character, with outstanding detail of sculpting around eyes and mouth made possible by larger size, fine quality bisque and painting, original body finish. $3000/4500

302. Rare German Bisque Character, 207, by Catterfelder Puppenfabrick
15" (38 cm.) Bisque socket head, painted facial features, almond shaped pale blue eyes in defined sockets, red and black upper eyeliner, single stroke curved brows, accented eye corners, tiny nose with accented nostrils, closed mouth with center accent line, brunette mohair wig, composition and wooden ball-jointed body, antique costume. Condition: generally excellent. Marks: 25 207. Comments: Catterfelder Puppenfabrick, circa 1912. Value Points: rare model with well defined character expression, fine modeling around the eyes and cheeks, finest quality of bisque and painting. $3500/4500

303. German Bisque Pouting Character, 6970, by Gebruder Heubach
16" (41 cm.) Pink tinted bisque socket head, dark blue intaglio eyes with large black pupils white eye dots, short feathered brows, accented eye corners and nostrils, closed mouth in downcast pouting expression, accent line between the lips, brunette human hair wig, composition and wooden ball-jointed body, antique costume. Condition: generally excellent. Marks: 6970 6 Germany Heubach (sunburst). Comments: Gebruder Heubach, circa 1912. Value Points: appealing character with fine quality of bisque and painting, original body and body finish. $800/1200

304. German Bisque Character with Pouty Expression
13" (33 cm.) Solid domed bisque socket head with unusual glazed finish, painted small blue eyes with prominent black pupils, black upper eyeliner, short stroke brows, accented nostrils, closed mouth with pouting lips, brunette mohair wig, composition and wooden ball-jointed body, antique costume. Condition: generally

excellent, few wig pulls at back of head. Marks: A (script) 3. Comments: attributed to Dressel, circa 1910. Value Points: rare model with unusual decorative glaze on complexion enhances the character expression. $1200/1800

305. German Bisque Brown-eyed Character by Hertel and Schwab

14" (36 cm.) Bisque socket head, painted facial features, brown eyes with white eyedots, black and red upper eyeliner, short feathered brows, accented nostrils and eye corners, closed mouth with defined space between the outlined lips, brunette mohair wig, composition and wooden ball-jointed body, antique costume.

Condition: generally excellent, small cheek rub. Marks: 141 3. Comments: Hertel and Schwab, circa 1912. Value Points: hard to find model with appealing brown eyes, excellent sculpting details. $1800/2500

306. Rare German Bisque Character, 520, by Bahr and Proschild for Kley and Hahn

18" (46 cm.) Bisque socket head, painted pale blue eyes, black upper eyeliner with very lightly fringed brows, accented nostrils and eye corners, closed mouth with slightly smiling expression, accented lips, auburn mohair wig, composition and wooden ball-jointed body, antique costume and leather ankle boots. Condition: generally excellent. Marks: 520 6 (head) Heinrich Handwerck Germany (body). Comments: Bahr and Proschild for Kley and Hahn, circa 1910. Value Points: rare model with most endearing expression, wonderful quality of bisque and painting, original body finish. $3500/4500

block shaped feet, the entire body covered by black flannel suit with attached orange flannel mittened jacket, simple wind-up device hidden in torso causes him to sway back and forth. Condition: good, surface dust and very slight spots. Marks: Oswald, United Universal Pictures Corp, An Irwin toy (cloth label) Darling Toddler, Wind me up and I will Walk, An Irwin Product (paper label). Comments: circa 1928, designed by Disney for the Universal Studios series; after legal hassles with Universal, Disney went to create his own Mickey Mouse. Value Points: extremely rare early comic film character with original labels. $3000/4000

307. German Bisque Pouty, "Phillip" by Kammer and Reinhardt in Fine Larger Size
24" (60 cm.) Bisque socket head, blue glass sleep eyes, painted dark curly lashes, feathered brows, accented nostrils, closed mouth with downcast lips in pouting expression, center accent line, blonde mohair bobbed wig, composition and wooden fully-jointed toddler body with side-hip jointing, antique undergarments. Condition: generally excellent. Marks: K*R S&H 115/A 60. Comments: Kammer and Reinhardt, circa 1912. Value Points: very fine quality of modeling and bisque, lustrous complexion patina, original body and body finish, with vintage Steiff duck and flannel felt slippers. $3500/4500

308. Very Rare American Cloth "Oswald the Lucky Bunny"
13" (33 cm.) 18" including ears. A stuffed flannel figure with applied face having stitched nose and painted facial features, pie-shaped eyes, wide beaming smile has large brown flannel ears with orange flannel lining, carton torso with wire arms and upper legs, cylinder legs,

309. German Mohair "Eric" by Steiff
6" (15 cm.) Cream and tan mohair bat with armature arms and legs allowing for posing, black bead eyes and nose, two layer felt ears with painted shading, with original shaded fabric bat wings. With original yellow tag, 1317, silver button, and paper label "Eric". Steiff, Germany, circa 1960. Excellent condition. $300/400

310. German Bisque Pouting Character, 115A, by Kammer and Reinhardt with Teddy Bear
12" (30 cm.) Bisque socket head, small blue glass sleep eyes, painted curly lashes, short feathered brows, accented nostrils, closed mouth with downcast pouting lips, blonde human hair braids, composition and wooden ball-jointed toddler body with side-hip jointing, antique dress, undergarments, shoes. Condition: generally excellent. Marks: I K*R Simon & Halbig 115/A 30. Comments: Kammer and Reinhardt, circa 1912, from their art character reform series. Value Points: rarer small character with deeply sculpted features, fine bisque, original toddler body, carrying very loved and worn little early teddy. $2500/3500

311. German Bisque Child, 1269, by Simon & Halbig in Original Costume
31" (79 cm.) Bisque socket head, blue glass sleep eyes, thick dark eyeliner, painted curly lashes, incised eyeliner, rose blushed eye shadow, slightly modeled brush-stroked brows with decorative glaze, accented eye corners, shaded nostrils, open mouth, accented lips, four porcelain teeth, pierced ears, blonde mohair wig, composition and wooden ball-jointed body. Condition: generally excellent. Marks: S&H 1269 Dep Germany 15. Comments: Simon & Halbig, circa 1900. Value Points: rare model with lovely bisque and painting, original wig, body, body finish, beautiful antique costume of rose sateen that is likely original. $1200/1700

312. A Well-Loved Early German Mohair Teddy by Steiff
16" (41 cm.) Golden mohair teddy with swivel head, long snout nose, stitched ears, black shoe-button eyes, embroidered brown nose and mouth, excelsior stuffed body with characteristic back hump, elongated jointed arms, hip-jointed legs with large feet, felt paw pads. Well-loved condition with sparse mohair on face, stuffing lacking in upper arms, felt paw pads worn, Steiff silver button in ear. Steiff, Germany, circa 1910. $800/1000

313. Very Large German Bisque Child by Heinrich Handwerck in Antique Boy's Suit

40" (102 cm.) Bisque socket head, blue glass sleep eyes, dark painted curly lashes, brushstroked brows with feathered highlights, accented eye corners and nostrils, open mouth, shaded and accented lips, four porcelain teeth, pierced ears, brunette wig, composition and wooden ball-jointed body. Condition: generally excellent. Marks: Germany Heinrich Handwerck Simon & Halbig 9. Comments: Handwerck, circa 1900. Value Points: rare large child doll has lovely bisque and painting, wears antique boy's suit and cap. $1800/2500

314. American Tin Lithographed Mechanical "Hercules" Ferris Wheel

17" (43 cm.) Lithographed tin ferris wheel with brilliantly colored designs and scenes of children has six swinging cars and, when wound, the wheel revolves and the cars swing back and forth. American, circa 1940. Excellent condition. $300/500

315. American Tin Lithographed "Milton Berle Car" in Original Box

6" (15 cm.) A fantastical tin lithographed car with comical decals such as "Hey Mom, I'm drivin' fancy", has two large back wheels and two small front wheels, Milton Berle figure with oversized hat in the driver's seat. When wound, the car twists and turns eccentrically. Excellent condition, virtually unplayed with in original colorful box (one flap missing). Louis Marx, circa 1950s. $500/800

316. American Tin Lithographed Mechanical "Pinocchio" by Marx

8" (20 cm.) Standing lithographed tin figure of Pinocchio with painted classic Disney costume has moveable eyes, and separately hinged over-sized feet. When wound, his eyes blink and he totters side to side. Marked C. 1939 Disney, Louis Marx. and

Pinocchio on his hat. Very good condition, slight paint wear on nose, functions well. Marx, circa 1940. $400/500

317. American Tin Lithographed "Charlie McCarthy" by Marx in Original Box
8" (20 cm.) Standing tin lithographed figure of Charlie McCarthy with classic gentleman's formal costume, his name printed on the top hat, having hinged jaw and oversized feet. When wound, his jaw moves frantically up and down as though talking rapidly, and he sways from side to side. Marked "Marx" on the back, and preserved in original box with illustrations of Edgar Bergen and Charlie. Excellent condition. Marx, circa 1940s. $500/700

318. American Passenger Train Set, 347, by Lionel in Original Boxes
14" (36 cm.) cars. The set comprises three cars, #309 red Pullman New York Lines, #312 red Lionel Lines Observation, and olive green #8E engine, in their original individual boxes, and in large outer box with illustrations and advertising. Along with an additional Lionel Lines platform car with two brass searchlights. Excellent near mint unplayed with condition. Lionel, circa 1930. $800/1200

319. English Tin/Celluloid Mechanical Wind-up "Mickey and Minnie Hand Car in Original Box
7" (18 cm.) A tin red handcar with cast iron wheels and amusing illustrations of Mickey has celluloid Mickey and Minnie with jointed tin arms posed on either end of the pumping lever, and when wound, they "pump" the hand-car and move along the included metal tracks. The toy is presented in its (very worn) original box, along with the original packaging house and station for Mickey and Minnie with colorful illustrations. Labeled Brimtoy Brand, British Made, and Wells London. Toy in excellent condition. Circa 1940s. $800/1000

In 1925 Arch and Hazel Baranger and inventor Robert Gerlach created the Baranger Studios in Pasadena, California with the purpose of creating amusing mechanical vignettes to be used as promotional pieces in jewelry stores. Known as motion displays, the imaginative pieces were designed to capture the attention of passers-by while simultaneously promoting the notion of acquiring diamonds, jewelry or watches. Small retailers in towns and small cities around America could subscribe to the Baranger Studio service whereby each month they would receive a new "motion display" to place in their store window, sending the former display back to Baranger who would forward it to another store in a round robin manner. From 1925 to 1959 the Baranger Studios created more than 250 different displays whose amusing figures performed imaginatively in their little theatre settings.

320. American Motion Display "Alice" by Baranger
19" (48 cm.) Arranged upon a textured platform is a closed book with an open book placed atop it; a young girl, Alice, is seated upon the closed book appearing to peer at the open pages in which different characters and sayings pop up and down as different pages are "turned", such as Tweedle Dee & Dum ("Which Twin 'ill Win?"), the King, the Jack ("It Takes a Diamond to Win a Heart") and Humpty Dumpty. The White Rabbit peeks over the top of the book. American, Baranger, circa 1925. $5000/7500

321. American Motion Display "Gem Mine" by Baranger

19" (48 cm.) A sculpted rock formation has various openings in which eight different miners are toiling, while a diamond shuttle goes up and down delivering diamonds to the hand-car labeled "gems from mine to you" that revolves around the track. The miners all perform various tasks when activated. Excellent condition. American, Baranger, circa 1935. $5000/7500

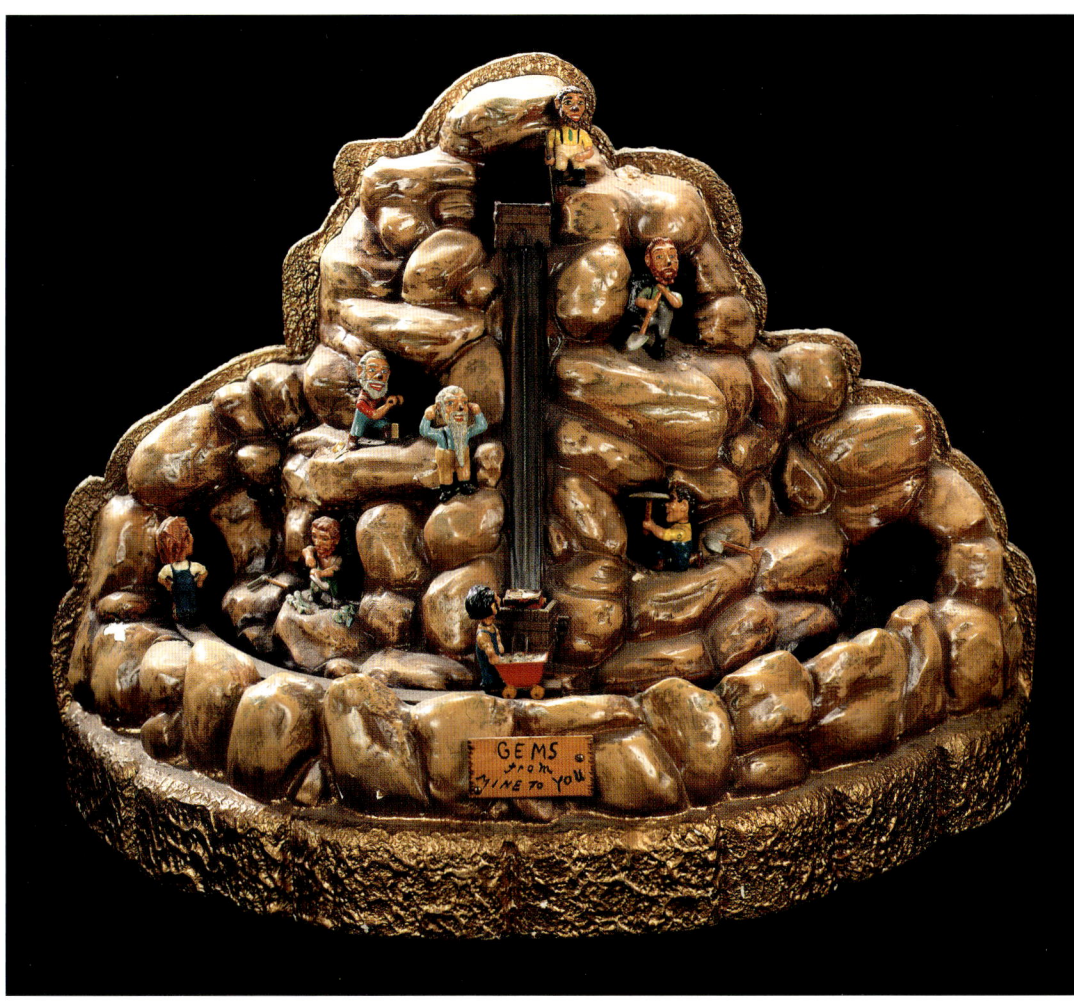

322. American Motion Display "Wrist Watch" by Baranger Studios

13" (33 cm.) A box-shaped base displays a propped up wrist watch whose crystal is being held open by a diligent worker while another watch maker winds the knob back and forth. Three other watch makers perform various moving tasks including one that peeks in and out from the second-hand hole in which he is hiding. Excellent condition. Baranger, circa 1935. $5000/7500

323. Pretty German Bisque Doll with Closed Mouth by Kestner
17" (43 cm.) Bisque socket head, blue glass sleep eyes, painted lashes, rose blushed eye shadow, brush-stroked feathered brows, accented nostrils and eye corners, closed mouth with impressed dimples at lip corners, blonde mohair wig over plaster pate, early composition and wooden fully-jointed body. Condition: generally excellent. Marks: VIII. Comments: Kestner, circa 1890. Value Points: beautiful bisque with luminous patina on the closed mouth child, wonderful antique costume, original body and body finish. $1200/1700

324. Large German Bisque Child with Closed Mouth by Kestner
28" (71 cm.) Bisque socket head, brown glass sleep eyes, dark eyeliner, dark curlylashes, incised upper eyeliner, thick brush-stroked brows with decorative glaze, accented nostrils, closed mouth with outlined lips, dimpled chin, brunette human hair over plaster pate, composition and wooden ball-jointed body, wearing antique silk dress, fancy bonnet, undergarments, leather shoes. Condition: generally excellent. Marks: L 1/2 made in Germany 15 1/2. Comments: Kestner, circa 1890. Value Points: beautiful bisque with richly painted features on the closed mouth doll, original body finish, lovely old wig. $2200/2800

325. English Porcelain Figure "Punch and Judy Man" by Royal Doulton
9" (23 cm.) One piece figure of puppeteer standing and holding classic Punch and Judy figures in his hands, while he admires them. Marked Royal Doulton. The figure was made for ten years from 1980-1990. Excellent condition. $400/700

326. English Porcelain Seated Alice with Book by Royal Doulton
5" (13 cm.) One piece porcelain figure of modestly seated Alice in Wonderland with blue dress, blonde hair with white band, holding book in her lap. Marked Royal Doulton. The figure was created from 1960-1980. Excellent condition. $200/300

327. German Bisque Closed Mouth Child, X, by Kestner
14" (36 cm.) Bisque socket head, blue glass sleep eyes, dark eyeliner, painted lashes, brush-stroked and feathered brows, accented nostrils, closed mouth with downcast pouting lips, accent line between the lips, blonde mohair wig over plaster pate, early composition and wooden fully-jointed body with straight wrists, antique cream costume, shoes, straw bonnet. Condition: generally excellent. Marks: X. Comments:

Kestner, circa 1885. Value Points: very dear expression on the wistful faced child, fine quality of bisque, original body and body finish. $2000/2500

328. Collection of 22 Royal Doulton Figures, Mostly Beatrix Potter
3" (8 cm.) -4". Each is one piece porcelain figure with amusingly detailed people-like pose and costume, including 17 Beatrix Potter figures, of which Jemima Puddleduck, Peter Rabbit, Mrs. Tittlemouse, Samuel Whiskers, and Benjamin Bunny are from the 1940s; Flopsy, Mopsy and Cottontail, Mrs. Rabbit, Johnny Town-Mouse, and Old Lady in a Shoe are from the 1950s, and 8 others are from the 1970s. Also included is "Bunnykins Family Photograph" of 1973, and 4 Wood mouses from the Brambley House Gift Collection for Royal Doulton, after the books by Jill Barklem, 1980s. Excellent condition. $600/900

149

329. Six Porcelain Girls by Royal Doulton

6" (15 cm.) tallest. Each is one piece porcelain figure of dainty girl in graceful pose, including Dink-Doo, Sweeting, Ivy, Mary had a Little Lamb, Lavinia, and Toodles. Marked Royal Doulton. Circa 1930s. Excellent condition. $400/600

330. Rare German Bisque Character "Baby Bo-Kaye"

16" (41 cm.) h. 11" circ. Solid domed bisque head with flanged neck, brown sculpted baby hair with low swept curls across the forehead, brown glass sleep eyes, painted lashes, tinted brows, accented nostrils, closed mouth with downcast lips, very plump cheeks, muslin body, composition lower limbs, antique costume. Condition: bisque excellent, body

is original albeit paint flaking on composition. Marks: copr. by J.L. Kallus Germany. Comments: rare model designed by American artist, Joseph Kallus, patron of Rose O'Neill, and marketed as Baby Bo-Kaye, produced in Germany, circa 1925. $1200/1800

331. Tiny French All-Bisque Mignonette with Wooden Lambs in Presentation Box

3" (8 cm.) x 4" box. 2 1/2" doll. All bisque doll with swivel head, painted facial features, brunette hair, peg-jointed bisque arms and legs, painted pale blue boots, is presented in original box, along with six tiny wooden lambs, all still tied into box with colorful engraving on the lid, with original silk rose ribbons. Excellent condition. French, circa 1890. $400/600

332. German All-Bisque Doll with Bare Feet
5" (13 cm.) Solid domed bisque swivel head, blue glass sleep eyes, painted dark curly lashes, lightly feathered brows, accented nostrils, closed mouth with downcast lips, brunette mohair braids, peg-jointed bisque arms and legs, nicely costumed. Condition: generally excellent. Comments: circa 1885, possibly Kling. Value Points: very beautiful all bisque with swivel head, wonderful detail of muscular legs, bare feet. $600/800

333. Exceptional Bisque Portrait Mannequin
39" (99 cm.) Bisque mannequin head with oval-shaped face, well defined facial lines, blue glass inset

eyes, delicately painted lashes and brows, eyeliner, accented nostrils and eye corners, closed mouth with center accent line, brunette mohair wig, on mannequin body with wooden articulated arms, wearing antique costume. Condition: professional overpaint on complexion although original painting retained on facial features, wooden arms repainted. Marks: P. Imans Paris (body). Comments: circa 1915, mystery maker of the portrait head, probably Simon and Halbig, on French Imans mannequin body. Value Points: exceptionally beautiful model with serene expression is very rare. $5000/7500

332.1. German Bisque Three-Faced Doll by Carl Bergner
13" (33 cm.) Bisque socket head with variant faces depicting, alternately, crying, laughing or sleeping child, the former two with blue glass eyes, and each with closed mouth and beaded teeth, painted lashes, brush-stroked brows, shaded and accented nostrils, a cardboard hood enclosing the back of head and "hidden" faces, carton torso, composition limbs, lace costume. Condition: generally excellent. Marks: C.B. Comments: Carl Bergner, circa 1890, the various faces are revealed by turning knob at top of head. Value Points: original body, fine quality of bisque and decoration including "tear" on crying face. $1100/1500

334. French Bisque Bébé Jumeau, Incised Depose Model
16" (41 cm.) Pressed bisque socket head, brown glass paperweight inset eyes, lushly painted lashes, rose blushed eye shadow, brush-stroked and multi-feathered brows, accented nostrils, closed mouth with outlined lips, pierced ears, blonde mohair wig over cork pate. Condition: generally excellent. Marks: Depose Jumeau 7 (incised, with artist checkmarks) Jumeau Medaille d'Or Paris (body). Comments: Emile Jumeau, circa 1885, the model was made for one year only. Value Points: fine creamy bisque with appealing shy expression original body and body finish, antique lace dress, undergarments, French cream kidskin shoes signed with full figure of doll. $3500/4500

335. French Bisque Bébé E.J. by Jumeau, Size 4
14" (36 cm.) Pressed bisque socket head, brown glass paperweight inset eyes, painted lashes, rose blushed eye shadow, feathered brows, accented nostrils and eye corners, closed mouth with outlined lips, pierced ears, blonde mohair wig over cork pate, French composition fully-jointed body. Condition: generally excellent, body is by Steiner, but appropriately sized and of the same era. Marks: Depose E. 4 J. (and artist checkmarks, head). Comments: Emile Jumeau, circa 1884. Value Points: rarer size E.J. with very fine modeled and quality of bisque, lovely antique costume, pink kidskin Jumeau shoes, straw bonnet, original body finish. $3500/4500

336. French Brown-Complexioned Bisque Bébé by Steiner, Figure A
12" (30 cm.) Brown-complexioned bisque socket head, brown glass paperweight inset eyes, black painted lashes, black brush-stroked and multi-feathered brows, accented nostrils, open mouth, four porcelain teeth, pierced ears, black mohair fleecy wig, French composition and wooden fully-jointed body. Condition: generally excellent. Marks: A 5 Le Parisien Bte SGDG (head) Bébé Le Parisien Medaille d'Or Paris (body). Comments: Jules Steiner, circa 1888. Value Points: pretty golden brown complexion, original wig, body, body finish, factory muslin chemise dress. $2200/2800

337. Outstanding French Bisque Earliest Period EJ, Size 11
24" (61 cm.) Pressed bisque socket head with very full cheeks, strong throat, brown glass paperweight inset eyes, thick dark eyeliner, painted delicate lashes, mauve blushed eye shadow, delicately feathered brows, accented eye corners, shaded nostrils, closed mouth with defined space between the outlined lips, separately modeled pierced ears, (frail) original lambswool wig over cork pate, French composition and wooden eight-loose-ball-jointed body with plump lower arms, straight wrists. Condition: generally excellent, flake at right pierced ear hole. Marks: EJ 11 (head) Jumeau Medaille d'Or Paris (body, Comments: Emile Jumeau, circa 1880, the earliest period of his signature bébé. Value Points: rare large early bébé with gorgeous sculpting, finest quality bisque and painting, original body with original finish, included is antique velvet and silk dress, leather shoes, and antique blonde mohair wig. $12,000/15,000

338. Early French Bisque Bébé Schmitt, Size 1, Known as "Cup and Saucer" Style
15" (38 cm.) Pale bisque head with flat-cut socket head that swivels upon paper mache torso neck, rounded facial modeling, almond shaped blue glass enamel inset eyes with spiral threading, dark eyeliner, painted curly lashes, lightly feathered brows, accented eye corners and nostrils of tiny pertly shaped nose, closed mouth with center accent line, pierced ears, blonde lambswool wig original Schmitt pate signed "1", original composition and wooden eight-loose-ball-jointed body with flat-cut derriere, nicely costumed in antique silks. Condition: generally excellent. Marks: 1 Bte SGDG (head). Comments: Schmitt et Fils, circa 1878, earliest model of that firm's bisque bébé. Value Points: very beautiful example whose dramatic eyes contrast the plump sculpting and delicate bisque, original body and body finish, early neck style. $8000/12,000

339. French Fashion Costumes for Petite Poupée, 1870 Era
For petite lady-body poupée about 12"-13". Comprising three costumes and a taupe flannel wool cape with yarn tassels. The costumes include a grey flannel two piece gown with brown silk trim; aqua cotton sateen flowered gown with three tiers of pleated skirts, bustle and maroon silk bow, and delicate rose and cream striped two-piece gown with tiered pleated skirt. Excellent condition. Circa 1870. $800/1000

340. French Bisque Bébé, Size 11, by Gaultier Freres
30" (76 cm.) Bisque socket head, large blue glass paperweight inset eyes, dark eyeliner, rose painted eye shadow, painted dark curly lashes, accented eye corners, shaded nostrils, closed mouth with accented lips, pierced ears, French composition and wooden fully-jointed body. Condition: generally excellent. Marks: 11 F.G. (scroll). Comments: Gaultier Freres, circa 1888. Value Points: beautiful large eyes enhance the lovely creamy complexion, fine maroon velvet frock, ivory silk bonnet, leather ankle boots. $3500/4500

341. Rare French Bisque Block Letter Bébé by Gaultier in Size 16
42" (107 cm.) Bisque socket head, brown glass paperweight inset eyes, dark eyeliner, painted lashes, widely arched

brush-stroked and feathered brows, accented eye corners, shaded nostrils, closed mouth with outlined lips, pierced ears, impressed lip and chin dimples, brunette human hair wig, French composition and wooden fully jointed body, lovely antique costume. Condition: generally excellent. Marks: F 16 G. (block letters). Comments: Gaultier, circa 1884. Value Points: very rare large size of the early block letter Gaultier bébé enhanced with lovely delicate bisque, original body and body finish. $9000/13,000

342. Petite French Bisque Bebe Bru Jne R with Kiss-throwing Mechanism

11" (28 cm.) Bisque socket head, tiny blue glass inset eyes, painted lashes, feathered fringed brows, accented eye corners, closed mouth with center accent line, pierced ears, blonde mohair wig over cork pate, French composition and wooden fully jointed body with pull-string kiss-throwing mechanism, nicely costumed. Condition: generally excellent. Marks: Bru JneR 2. Comments: Bru, circa 1895. Value Points: petite closed mouth bebe with original body. $3000/4000

343. German All-Bisque Miniature Doll with Black Complexion by Kuhnlenz

6" (15 cm.) Ebony black bisque socket head on black bisque torso, black glass inset eyes, painted black brows and lashes with decorative glaze, closed mouth with coral shaded lips, black fleecy hair, loop-jointed ebony black bisque arms and legs with bare feet. Condition: generally excellent. Marks: 61-14 (head and limbs). Comments: Gebruder Kuhnlenz, circa 1890. Value Points: rare model with fine characterization, beautiful complexion. $600/900

344. German Brass Miniature Doll Bed by Maerklin

6" (15 cm.) The brass bed features curved head and foot boards with spindled insets and gracefully curved scrolls at the sides, original coiled springs, nicely fitted with antique linens and covers. Excellent condition. Germany, circa 1890, Maerklin. $400/500

345. Petite French Bisque Bebe Bru Jne R with Closed Mouth

13" (33 cm.) Bisque socket head, blue glass paperweight inset eyes, painted lashes, brush-stroked and feathered brows, accented nostrils and eye corners, closed mouth with outlined lips, pierced ears, blonde mohair wig over cork pate, French composition and wooden fully-jointed body, silk dress in the antique style. Condition: generally excellent, head and body (unsigned Jumeau) not original albeit of the period and appropriately sized. Marks: Bru JneR 3. Comments: Bru, circa 1892. Value Points: pretty closed mouth petite bebe with deep blue eyes. $3000/4000

346. Rare German Bisque Taufling Baby in Antique Costume

15" (38 cm.) Solid domed bisque head with flat-cut neck socket that pivots on shoulder plate neck dowel, sculpted brown hair with curly details, sculpted ears, painted facial features, blue eyes, red and black upper eyeliner, short stroke brows, accented nostrils and eye corners, closed mouth with center accent line, muslin midriff with bellows crier, porcelain hips and lower limbs with painted black shoes. Condition: hairlines on left arm and legs, original firing lines on head seam. Comments: Germany, circa 1860, the doll combines rare glazed bisque head with porcelain shoulder plate and limbs that are original together. Value Points: very rare taufling baby with superb sculpting detail, wearing original pique baby gown, undergarments, bonnet. $1200/1800

347. Very Beautiful French Bisque Bebe E.J. by Jumeau, Size 12
26" (66 cm.) Pressed bisque socket head, very full lower cheeks, deep blue glass paperweight inset eyes, thick black eyeliner, rose blushed eye shadow, lushly painted lashes, brush-stroked and multi-feathered brows, accented nostrils and eye corners, closed mouth with shaded and outlined lips, separately modeled applied ears, blonde mohair wig over cork pate, French composition and wooden fully-jointed body with straight wrists, wearing lovely antique lace dress, undergarments, shoes, straw bonnet. Condition: generally excellent. Marks: Depose E 12 J (head). Jumeau Medaille d'Or Paris (body). Comments: Emile Jumeau, circa 1885. Value Points: gorgeous model of the deposed bebe with finest luminous complexion, very large eyes with dramatic painting of eye shadow and lashes, fine large size. $7500/9500

348. French Bisque "Eden Bebe", Size 16, with Character Expression
32" (81 cm.) Bisque socket head with pale complexion, deep blue glass paperweight inset eyes, thick dark eyeliner, painted dark lashes, widely arched feathered brows, accented eye corners, shaded nostrils, open mouth, shaded and outlined lips, row of tiny porcelain teeth, pierced ears, blonde mohair wig, French composition and wooden fully-jointed body. Condition: generally excellent. Marks: Eden Bebe Paris 16 (head)

Bebe Jumeau Diplome d'Honneur (body). Comments: circa 1895. Value Points: wonderfully characterized expression enhanced by unusually fine quality of bisque and painting for this model, wearing early muslin chemise, signed leather boots. $3500/4500

349. French Paper Mache Character by Roullet & Decamps
14" (36 cm.) Paper mache head with highly characterized facial model painted features with blue eyes, widely beaming smile, pointy nose, and blushed cheeks and eye shadow, brunette human hair, carton torso and limbs, wire upper arms and legs. Condition: generally excellent. Comments: Roullet & Decamps, circa 1910, when wound, the little doll sways her body from side to side, turns her head and appears to "rock" the little baby in her arms. Value Points: fine original condition, wearing original costume. $1200/1500

350. French Bisque Automaton attributed to Renou
16" (41 cm.) Standing upon a red velvet covered platform is a bisque head doll with bright blue glass eyes, painted lashes and brows, accented nostrils and eye corners, open mouth, teeth, pierced ears, auburn

mohair wig, carton torso, wire upper arms and legs, bisque hands. Condition: generally excellent. Marks: F.G. (scroll, on doll). Comments: attributed to Renou, circa 1895, when wound, two tunes play, the doll turns her head side to side and alternately lifts her arms. Value Points: pristine condition, the little girl wears rich rose silk satin dress, lace edged silk apron, lovely music. $3000/4000

351. German Bisque "Sunshine Baby" by Louis Wolf

17" (43 cm.) Solid domed bisque socket head with very plump cheeks, tan baby hair with softly sculpted curls, small blue glass sleep eyes, tan tinted brows, painted lashes, accented nostrils, closed mouth, composition bent limb baby body with distinctively shaped fingers, well costumed. Condition: generally excellent. Marks: Germany Sunshine Baby L.W. & Co. Inc 7. Comments: circa 1925, made in Germany for the American market. Value Points: rare model with well defined and distinctive features. $400/600

352. Set, German Bisque Quintuplets by Herm Steiner

8" (20 cm.) Each has bisque head with painted baby hair and tinted brows, tiny glass sleep eyes, painted lashes, closed mouth, muslin body, composition hands. Condition: generally excellent. Marks: HS (intertwined 15 Germany. Comments: Herm Steiner, circa 1925. Value Points: the little matching babies are costumed in muslin baby gowns, with pink and blue flannel robes. $1200/1500

one with glass eyes, mohair wigs, antique costumes. Condition: generally excellent. Comments: Germany, circa 1900. Value Points: fine and hard to find doll house accessory. $400/600

355. Small German Bisque Character, "Hans" by Kammer and Reinhardt
9" (23 cm.) Bisque socket head, painted facial features, blue eyes, one stroke brows, accented nostrils and eye corners, closed mouth with pouty lips, center accent line, brunette mohair wig, five piece composition body, painted shoes. Condition: generally excellent.

353. Very Large French Bisque Bebe Steiner, Figurer A, Size 20
34" (86 cm.) Bisque socket head, blue glass paperweight inset eyes, dark eyeliner, painted lashes, thickly brush-stroked fringed brows, accented eye corners, shaded nostrils, closed mouth with shaded and outlined lips, defined chin and philtrum dimples, pierced ears, brunette human hair, Steiner composition fully-jointed body with straight wrists, wearing lovely antique silk dress, undergarments, lace bonnet. Condition: generally excellent. marks: J. Steiner Bte SGDG Paris Fre A 20. Comments: Jules Steiner, circa 1888. Value Points: rare large model with gorgeous luminous quality of bisque, fine sculpting, original body. $6000/8500

354. German Tin Lithographed Miniature Garden Setting with Bisque Dolls
11" (28 cm.) l. x 6"d. Arranged upon a tin lithographed platform to simulate garden grass is a tin trellis decorated with flowers and furnished with tin garden bench, table and two chairs, and peopled with three bisque dolls, two with painted features and

Marks: K*R 114. Comments: Kammer and Reinhardt, circa 1912, their model marketed as "Hans". Value Points: well modeled features on the small model, wearing original gentleman's formal wear suit. $800/1200

356. German Bisque Laughing Character, 6971, by Gebruder Heubach
16" (41 cm.) Pink tinted bisque socket head, painted facial features, intaglio side-glancing blue eyes, white eye dots, black upper eyeliner, one stroke brows, accented nostrils and eye corners, closed mouth modeled as though open and smiling, two beaded lower teeth, brunette human hair in side braids, composition and wooden ball-jointed body, pretty antique dress. Condition: generally excellent. Marks: 6971 Germany 5. Comments: Gebruder Heubach, circa 1912. Value Points: wonderful detail of sculpting on the laughing faced child. $800/1200

357. Two, German Bisque Characters by Kammer and Reinhardt
7" (18 cm.) and 7 1/2". Each has bisque socket head, painted facial features, blue eyes, closed mouth with pouting expression, blonde mohair wig, composition body, antique costume. Condition: generally excellent. Marks: K*R 101 (or 114). Comments: Kammer and Reinhardt, circa 1912, two characters "Marie" and "Gretchen" from their art character series. Value Points: fine quality of bisque and expressive features, original body. $1200/1500

358. Exceptional German Bisque Child, 939, by Simon and Halbig
38" (97 cm.) Bisque socket head with long-faced modeling, full cheeks, brown glass sleep eyes, thick brush-stroked brows with feathered highlights, black eyeliner, painted lashes, accented eye corners, shaded nostrils, four porcelain teeth, slightly parted outlined lips, four porcelain teeth, pierced ears, (new) brunette wig, composition and wooden ball-jointed body, antique lace dress and velvet bonnet. Condition: generally excellent. Marks: S 18 H 939 Dep (head) Handwerck (body). Comments: Simon and Halbig, circa 1890. Value Points: beautiful large model of the rarer doll, has loveliest bisque and sculpting, defined dimples, original body and body finish. $2000/2500

359. Two German Porcelain Doll Heads
3.5" (9 cm.) Each is porcelain shoulder head with sculpted hair in ornate center-parted coiffure and painted facial features, one with midnight brown hair waved around face, with partially sculpted ears, into coiled braid at the back, and modeled bosom; the other with sculpted side wings of hair and elaborate chignon. Condition: generally excellent. Comments: Germany, circa 1865. Value Points: two early porcelain heads with rare coiffures. $400/500

361. German Porcelain Doll in Ornate Ceremonial Costume
7" (18 cm.) Porcelain shoulder head with black sculpted hair and painted facial features, painted beard, muslin body, porcelain limbs. Condition: generally excellent. Comments: circa 1885. Value Points: the doll is wearing elaborate ceremonial costume with jeweled crown, and holds tiny all-porcelain doll. $300/400

360. Lovely French Silk Poupee Dress
To fit plump bodied poupee about 15". Of finely patterned striped silk the gown features flared sides and coat sleeves, and is decorated with ice blue silk cotton sateen stitched-down pleats, with lace sleevelets and collar, tiny silver buttons. Excellent condition. Circa 1865. $500/800

362. Two, Early Porcelain Dolls for the French Market
8" (20 cm.) and 10". Each has porcelain shoulder head with black sculpted boyish hair, one with pink tinted complexion, each with painted facial features, blue eyes, tiny closed mouth, and each with original French kid hand-stitched body with shapely torso and one piece limbs, mitten hands. Condition: generally excellent. Comments: for the French market, circa 1865. Value Points: pleasing petite pair with rare boyish hair styles, antique costumes. $500/700